Horses of the Great War

Horses of the Great War

The Story in Art

John Fairley

Pen & Sword
MILITARY

First published in Great Britain in 2015 by
Pen & Sword Military
an imprint of
Pen & Sword Books Ltd
47 Church Street
Barnsley
South Yorkshire
S70 2AS

Copyright © John Fairley 2015

ISBN 978 1 47384 826 9

A CIP catalogue record for this book is available from the British Library

Typeset in Ehrhardt by
Mac Style Ltd, Bridlington, East Yorkshire
Printed and bound in India by Replika Press Pvt. Ltd.

Pen & Sword Books Ltd incorporates the imprints of Pen & Sword Archaeology, Atlas, Aviation, Battleground, Discovery, Family History, History, Maritime, Military, Naval, Politics, Railways, Select, Transport, True Crime, and Fiction, Frontline Books, Leo Cooper, Praetorian Press, Seaforth Publishing and Wharncliffe.

For a complete list of Pen & Sword titles please contact
PEN & SWORD BOOKS LIMITED
47 Church Street, Barnsley, South Yorkshire, S70 2AS, England
E-mail: enquiries@pen-and-sword.co.uk
Website: www.pen-and-sword.co.uk

Contents

List of Illustrations

Acknowledgements

My thanks go first to the individuals and institutions named in the picture credits who have looked after and sought out for us these works of art, which have been largely hidden away for so long.

Then to the compilers of the many regimental histories, which contain the best available detail of the experiences of horsemen in the war. The war museums of the Empire also contain the most valuable personal testimonies.

In the vast literature on the Great War – and the splendid London Library has an entire floor devoted to the conflict – acknowledgement must be paid, above all, to the late Marquis of Anglesey's lifelong devotion to restoring the reputation of the cavalry, and to the cohort of vets who put together the great authoritative official history of the animals recruited into service in the war, of the care they received and the fates that overtook them.

On a personal note, Henry Wilson of Pen & Sword has been unstinting in his encouragement, Sian Phillips of Bridgeman Art has been tireless in helping me track down these pictures, and George Chamier a perceptive and supportive editor.

Preface

In the Canadian War Museum in Ottawa there is this extraordinary painting of a cavalry charge. The horses hurtle forward in disciplined lines. The glistening threat of the sabres is thrust across the canvas. Men have already been hurled out of the saddle. Horses, too, are stumbling to the ground.

For all the world, this could be a companion piece to Lady Butler's famous painting of the charge of the Scots Greys at Waterloo. But there are clues to its difference. The uniforms are khaki, not royal red; the headgear is trench tin helmets, not dragoon casquettes; there are bandoliers of bullets. For this is taking place more than a century after Lady Butler's scene. It is Alfred Munnings' picture of the Canadian Strathcona's Horse, with Lieutenant Gordon Flowerdew – in the foreground – leading the charge in March 1918 which halted what had been until then the remorseless advance of the great German spring offensive.

By 1918 the Great War had spawned a vast array of new lethal technology. The tank had made its debut across the trenches and no-man's-land of Flanders. There was gas, and underground mines. Aircraft were fighting each other in the skies and dropping bombs on enemy lines. Armoured cars had appeared. The artillery had developed massive guns with huge range and great accuracy. The machine gun had reached a new and implacable rapidity.

It is scarcely credible then that the great German assault of 1918, so close to achieving decisive success, should have been turned at a key point by the means portrayed in Munnings' painting – cold steel on horseback.

Lieutenant Flowerdew was to die in the battle, shot through both legs and the chest but, to the last, urging his men on with the cry 'Carry on boys! We have won.' He was awarded the Victoria Cross.

The battle at Moreuil Wood was the last throw in an attempt to close the gap between the British and French lines, thus preventing the Germans crossing the River Avre and breaking through to Amiens and the coast. Flowerdew had led his Strathcona's Horse at full gallop against a phalanx of machine guns, rifles and artillery and cut right through them, then turned and continued to sabre the remaining enemy. The Strathconas lost two thirds of their men and horses. But the German advance was halted.

Munnings' painting is the most spectacular refutation of the myth that the cavalry played no significant part in the Great War. Alfred Munnings had spent the winter and early spring of 1918 with the Canadian cavalry. Already blind in one eye and rejected by his Army medical board, he had been recruited by his artist friend Cecil Aldin into the Army Remount Service and from there was enlisted by Paul Konody, the *Observer* art critic, on behalf of the Canadian

The Charge of Flowerdew's Squadron, Sir Alfred Munnings. (*Canadian War Museum, Ottawa, Canada/Bridgeman Images*)

After the Recapture of Bapaume, Christopher Nevinson. (*Rochdale Art Gallery, Lancashire, UK/Bridgeman Images*)

Government, to go out to France with their cavalry. He was with them through the month-long March retreat, but still managed to create more than twenty pictures.

Munnings' appointment was part of a concerted effort by the British and Imperial governments to create a record of the war, with correspondents and artists selected and dispatched to almost all the theatres of war. Many of the painters had been distinguished equestrian artists, and it was inevitable that their eye was caught by the hundreds of thousands of horses meeting the demands of the various campaigns, whether in France, the deserts of Mesopotamia or the assault on the German colonies in Africa.

The first two official war artists were only appointed in April 1917, nearly three years into the conflict, in the wake of the growing sentiment that painters at home were not doing justice to the nature of the conflict. James McBey was sent out to Egypt, where he became attached to the Australian horsemen and produced some of the epic paintings of the desert war. William Orpen was sent to France. That same summer, two artists who had served at the Front and whose reputation was to be made by their war work, Paul Nash and Christopher Nevinson, both exhibited in London. Within weeks, along with Sir John Lavery and Eric Kennington, they were sent back to France as official artists. They were joined by Munnings and in the end by a score of other artists, including George Clausen and the intensely emotional Lieutenant Harold Septimus Power, who was attached to the Australian forces in France. His *Bringing up the Guns* became one of the most reproduced pictures of the War.

In the remaining fearful months of the War these painters produced the great body of work which records the courage and suffering not only of the men but also of the horses who endured so much alongside them.

The poetry of the Great War is still the most acute avenue into the sentiments which sustained the spirits and the courage of the soldiers. There is the anguish of Wilfred Owen ('My subject is War and the pity of War. The Poetry is in the pity'). But a patriotic love of England is truly the romantic weft which threads its way through this indelibly affecting verse.

Then there are the 'blue remembered hills' of Housman's Shropshire. Or John Freeman's:

> Happy is England in the brave that die …
> Happy in all her dark woods, green fields, towns,
> Her hills and rivers and her chafing sea.

Or the Middlesborough man, I. A. Williams, contemplating a Flanders graveyard:

> For English songs and English winds
> Are they that bred these English minds.

Or Nowell Oxland, from the Borders:

> And it's there that I'd be lying
> With the heather close at hand,
> And the curlews faintly crying
> Mid the wastes of Cumberland.

Some poets, like Jeffery Day, wrote of the new-found ecstasies of flight, lost in the clouds:

> At last the choking mists release their hold,
> And all the world is silver, blue and gold.

But the tens of thousands of horses, whose efforts and strengths and sufferings so engaged the painters, seemed to make little impact on that generation of poets. They were raised, perhaps, in those last years when horses were more than ever tuned and treated as machines – machines to haul buses and trams, pull barges on canals, even circle endlessly to drive the paddle steamers, and of course provide all the motive power on road and field. The horsemen themselves at the front were caring enough of their charges, and the cavalrymen – most famously General Jack Seely with his horse Warrior – were deeply attached to their chargers. But for most of the men at the front, the horses seem to have been merely a supply chain, engines, literally just horse power, although this is Julian Grenfell writing of the soldier waiting to go over the top:

> The horses show him nobler powers.
> O patient eyes, courageous hearts.

And Richard Aldington, waiting to go to France, mused on:

> Interminable squadrons of silver and blue horses
> Pace in long ranks the blank fields of heaven.

The paintings of the Great War – John Singer Sargent's line of gassed soldiers, Paul Nash's shattered landscape at Ypres, Percy Wyndham Lewis's bombardments – have become as emblematic as the poetry in fixing the War in the public imagination. But the painters did have a great fascination, too, for the horses all around them. There is a treasure trove of wonderful paintings in the War Museums of Britain, Australia, Canada, South Africa, largely unseen and forgotten, which record the daunting tasks and sacrifices demanded from the horses in Flanders, Palestine, Mesopotamia and the Balkans.

Many of these paintings are full of power and emotion as the horses are confronted with the extreme demands of the battlefield. Others are triumphant narratives or doleful records of loss and defeat. But together they make a significant contribution to the art and the story of the Great War.

Bringing up the Guns, Harold Power. *(Private Collection/ © Galerie Bilderwelt/ Bridgeman Images)*

Prologue

As the twentieth century opened, one of the central anomalies of the industrial revolution was at its most acute. The great new inventions – steam ships, the railways, the mills, the mechanisation of the factories – and the resulting huge increases in output and the trade of Empire, all in fact depended on greatly increased horse power. People and goods were disgorged at grand railway stations and sprawling marshalling yards. But from there onwards there was no alternative to the horse. The railways laid on horse buses for their passengers; every ounce of cargo had to be moved by horse or human power; horses were even used to shunt the trains.

Horses pulled the canal boats, delivered the mail and were the only form of city transport, with horse-drawn cabs, trams and carriages. Every form of distribution required horse power. By 1900 there were more horses than at any time in history on the streets of London – at least 300,000. They were sustained by an infrastructure of extraordinary organizational complexity and sophistication. Although the first automobiles, which were very soon to be the nemesis of the horse, were already butting slowly through the congestion of London, the vast array of horse-related services, stabling, shoeing, driving, caring, were at their apogee.

Alongside its new hotel in Paddington, the Great Western Railway Company built an equine hostelry of stables four storeys high. Here were housed five hundred of the thousand or more horses that were required to carry goods from the trains to their final destination. It was quite a palace, with arched white doorways and blue brick aisles, and the fastidious indulgence of housing its inhabitants by colour, the greys all together in one stable, the chestnuts in another, the bays in a third.

London was already becoming a commuter city, with office workers arriving by train from all over the Home Counties. But within the city, all surface transport was by horse. The two-horse buses and the two-horse trams – the rails permitting the latter to carry twice as many passengers – were transporting 300 million passengers a year at a penny, a penny farthing or a penny halfpenny a trip.

Then there were vast elements of infrastructure like the Road Car Company's yard at Farm Lane in Fulham, with horses kept on two storeys in the squads of eleven which were required to service each bus or tram – one team resting, the other doing two- or three-hour stints, changing over as the trams returned after trips to Spitalfields or Liverpool Street or Covent Garden. Some 3,000 horses served the Road Car company's routes, with an attendant army just as large of stablemen, farriers, vets and feed waggoners.

Timberhauling, L.D. Luard. (*Private collection*)

The buses and the trams had already started to push the cabmen into decline as quickly as the horse-drawn buses and trams themselves were to meet their fate. But there were still more than 10,000 two- and four-horse cabs operated by the lower life of the London horse world – the cabmen cluttered the magistrates' courts more than members of any other profession, two thousand or more per year being fined or imprisoned for some offence.

And at life's end it was still impossible to have a proper funeral without the black Flemish horses imported by Dottridges on East Road in the East End.

Though the dominance of the horse was fading on the streets and highways of Britain, horses – and indeed mules and donkeys – remained in 1914 the mainstay of the country's intricate and crucial canal system. Indeed, they were to remain important until well after the Second World War. The Shropshire Union Canal Company owned more than 450 horses, with similar numbers spread up through the Grand Union, the Leeds and Liverpool and the other inland navigation systems which snaked across England from Bristol all the way up to beyond Lancaster.

These thousands of animals towed barges, often driven only by shouts and orders from the bargee in the stern of the vessel or ridden by children sitting bareback astride their withers. There was an elaborate network of stables along all the canals, analogous to the old post horse system, where horses and mules could stay overnight or fresh animals could be found.

The horses themselves became extremely adept at coping with the demands of the canal system – when to stop for oncoming traffic, how to lean into the collar to get the massive loads under way, even how to jump over stiles as high as 2 feet 6 inches, which were a regular hazard on the towpaths of the Bedfordshire canals. Indeed, Constable's painting *The Leaping Horse* shows just such a challenging moment. These animals could haul massive loads: two horses in tandem could take on 100 tons of barge cargo. In fact, the canal horses were so essential to the war economy that relatively few of them were impressed into the Army.

Death came for the London horse with all the efficiency that characterized the organization of his working life. Tram horses lasted four years, omnibus horses five, cab horses at most six or seven; the great brewery horses, solicitously managed, lasted ten years or more, and the black Flemish horses of the funeral trade endured perhaps longest of all.

The largest of the dozen or so horse slaughterers' yards in London was Harrison Barbers in Wandsworth. It was truly 'Abandon hope all ye who enter here', for by Act of Parliament no horse which entered these portals was allowed to come out alive. Blindfolded, the poleaxe laid them out in minutes. Immediately the mane was hogged, the hair destined for mattresses and fishing lines, just the first stage in a remorselessly efficient recycling of the 20,000 or more animals who entered the Wandsworth gates every year. The hooves were cut off, the shoes going straight back to the farriers to be reshaped for another owner, the hoof itself going to the gluemakers.

The carcass was then slung up and the hide stripped, to be sold around the world for roofing cabs and carriages or even to make leather breeches. The meat was sliced off and boiled to be

The Blue Rider, Wassily Kandinsky. (*Buhrle Collection, Zurich, Switzerland/ Bridgeman Images*)

sold for cat and dog food. There must have been legions of London cat and dog lovers, for the Wandsworth works produced 70 tons of pet meat every week.

Finally, the skeletons were pressed and pounded to produce oil for dressing leather and wax for the candle makers. The bones were crushed for the fertiliser trade, though some were preserved for the button makers.

The process took only an hour: seventy or eighty horses every day of the week, day and night.

It was during these last years before the War that, as it had a century earlier with Stubbs and the Ferneleys, the horse assumed a central position in the development of painting. Wassily Kandinsky and Franz Marc founded the *Blue Rider Almanac*, which had horses not only in its title but in many of the most celebrated works they made. Their interest in and adulation for 'primitive' styles was to be one of the key influences on twentieth century art. Marc's *Little Yellow Horses* of 1912 was one of the most admired of the pictures in the Blue Rider exhibition of that year. The 'Blue Riders' gathered round them kindred spirits – nearly all of them interested in the use of the horse in art – Paul Klee, August Macke and others. Sadly, a number of them did not survive to paint the war horses. Macke was killed within days of the start of the war in the attack on Belgium. Marc was killed in front of Verdun in 1916, though some of the sketches he made in the war were eventually published.

In Paris, too, the avant-garde were devoted to painting the horse. Degas was as fascinated by horses as he was by the ballet. The pointilliste Georges Seurat, living next door to a circus, found the flying horses and the bareback lady riders a fine focus for his work. In the previous decade, Henri de Toulouse-Lautrec had haunted the racecourse, and Paul Gauguin, even in far off Tahiti, found the horses and their riders on a South Seas beach one of his most evocative subjects.

In the decade before the war, in London too, there was intense interest in painting the horse. Frank Calderon was able to establish a school entirely devoted to animal painting. Hubert von Herkomer had his own school in the rather unlikely location of Bushey in Hertfordshire, with the young Lucy Kemp-Welch as his star pupil. In January 1914, barely six months before war broke out, the Society of Animal Painters was formed in London, with Kemp-Welch as its President. The founder members included a number of artists who were to become the prime painters of the horses in the coming war, including Alfred Munnings and Lionel Edwards.

Kemp-Welch herself eschewed the painting of racehorses and concentrated on the draught and native British breeds, their varied work and tasks and the environments in which she found them – an excellent preparation for the Army horses to come.

The pre-war years were the heyday of the Slade School in London, where so many of the young war artists studied. Futurists, Vorticists, Cubists, all flourished. As the critic Frank Rutter wrote:

The Little Yellow Horses, Franz Marc. (Staatsgalerie, Stuttgart, Germany/Artothek/ Bridgeman Images)

Scornful of old ideals and traditions, young artists of talent were inclined in the days of peace to stand on their heads in an effort to be fresh, unconventional and original. The war set the best of them firmly on their feet. Eccentricities and extravagances were purified away in the fiery ordeal of modern battles. When the outworn conventions of the Royal Academy failed, on the whole, to convey any adequate impression of this mighty world conflict, young artists rose from the ranks, finding new methods of expression.

Chapter One

Recruiting the War Horses

Within hours of war's declaration, across the length and breadth of the country, an extraordinary network of agents slipped into action. These were drawn from the true horsemen of England – mostly ex-officers, masters of foxhounds, farriers, country gentlemen, even hunting parsons and knackers' men. They were primed to supply, with implacable efficiency, the one thing that England's armies needed most – horses.

Already on that first day of war, 4 August, notices were delivered to farmers, carriage men, carters and hackney men in all the counties of Britain and Ireland, to produce their horses the next day or at the latest on 6 August. There were gatherings on village greens, in railway yards, in the stable yards of great estates. The horses' owners came knowing already the unpalatable choice that faced them – produce the horses for sale to the agents of the Army Remount Service or see them seized anyway by compulsory purchase. Elizabeth Owen, then a schoolgirl, recalled the impact of the requisitions:

> We heard that the khaki men were coming to take away all the horses from the village. Everything in the village was done by horses. The station was about a mile and a half away, and the train was met by a brake drawn by horses. The milk was delivered by horses and the butter used to be collected from the farms and brought in by horses to the butter market. There was a farmer who had a lovely pair we called the prancers. He thought he would try and hide these horses, but the khaki men found them. They tied them all together on a long rope – I think there were about twenty – all horses we used to know and love and feed. Then they started trotting them out of the village, and as they went out of the village we were terribly sad.

The requisitions were indeed ruthless. The official war reporter Basil Clarke witnessed, in the first week of the war, people in a trap being stopped on the road and their horse being bought from its protesting owner and taken out of the shafts there and then. The trap itself was left at the nearest inn. George Orwell recorded seeing a London cabman burst into tears when the Army requisitioned his horse.

The process of acquiring horses for the Army had been well prepared. Agents were provided with a little black tin box, which contained a government cheque book and a written authority to commandeer any horse they thought fit. Within hours, on 4 August, they received telegrams telling them they were authorized to open the little black boxes and get to work.

AT THE FRONT!

Every fit Briton should join our brave men at the Front.

ENLIST NOW.

PUBLISHED BY THE PARLIAMENTARY RECRUITING COMMITTEE, LONDON (POSTER No. 84)

PRINTED BY E.S.&A. ROBINSON LD BRISTOL

At the Front!, Lionel Edwards. (*National Army Museum, London, UK*)

Purchase of Horses, Edwin Noble. (*Imperial War Museum, London, UK*)

The newspapers reported large numbers of onlookers in subdued mood. The buying and selling proceeded relentlessly through the afternoon and evening of the first day. By the end of the second day the Army had purchased or impressed 140,000 horses – perhaps one in ten of all the horses in England – and was already dispatching them to the rail yards and on to vast depots like Romney in the south of England, bound for France.

By December, 18,000 of them would already be dead: killed in action, exhausted or abandoned in the retreat from Mons and the first battle of Ypres. They were the first in a casualty list which was to surpass half a million by the war's end in the British Army alone. The French Army was to lose almost a million, the Germans and their allies even more.

By the time of the legendary Christmas football matches between the trenches in 1914, the realities of the new war were imposing themselves, not least on the men who had to find the horses to supply the depleted armies. The Army Remount Department reckoned there were fewer than 70,000 suitable horses left in England. And so the remarkably well-oiled and resourceful Department turned to its reserve plan. Three thousand miles away across the ocean, the United States of America disposed of, it was known,13 million horses. The whole land, from sea to shining sea, was worked by horses bred from the heavy stock of old Europe: Shires, Clydesdales, Ardennes and above all Percherons from France. Percheron crosses with lighter mares had proved uniquely fitted for the work on the Great Plains and in the West. These are the types which appear in the paintings of Remington and Stull and stare out of the remarkable photographs of thirty- and forty-horse teams pulling early combine harvesters in the fields of Kansas.

But now great numbers of them were required for France. British officers from the Remount Commission were despatched to establish four huge holding depots in the United States, and they then fanned out to start the voracious process of purchasing animals in every farm state across the Union. During the Boer War, only fifteen year earlier, the British Army had established close relations with the major horse dealers in America. Indeed, one firm alone, the Guyton and Harrington Mule Company, had supplied more than 100,000 animals for South Africa. Now these arrangements were reactivated. They were on an enormous scale.

One depot in Kentucky stretched over 35 square miles and could accommodate 25,000 horses and mules. A rail link ran directly into the estate. There were innumerable paddocks, stables and veterinary hospitals, as well as the strictest security – German agents were suspected of the most dastardly ruses, including putting infected water into the drinking supply and even manufacturing little spiked bits of metal to be dropped into the horse feed.

The project was on a mammoth scale. Captain John Blakeway arrived in Columbia, Tennessee and within eight months had bought 16,388 horses and mules and sent them on their way to France, before moving on to sweep up the available stock in Missouri. The process, like so much of the Army Remount's work, was efficient beyond imagining. The animals were loaded on to trains from all over America and taken to the main holding depots, where they were first approved as fit to travel onward. No horse was allowed to be on a train for more than 36 hours, so further smaller rail-side holding depots had to be built.

The Straw Ride, Lucy Kemp-Welch. *(Imperial War Museum, London, UK)*

Finally they got to the East Coast, where they were again held for seven weeks to ensure they were clear of influenza before boarding specially converted ships, up to two thousand at a time. The determined care with which the horses were treated produced astonishing results. Throughout the war, only one animal in a hundred died on the Atlantic voyage, and nearly half the ships arrived without any deaths at all. In 1918 there were nearly two hundred crossings.

The plains and prairies of Canada and North America were to be the greatest source of horses, by far, throughout the war. The scale of the operation set in train by the British War Office was on an almost unimaginable scale. Three quarters of a million animals –768,572, to be precise – were bought in the four years of war to be shipped to the battlefields of France and Flanders. More than sixty vets and dozens of officers from the Army Remount Commission scoured the farm country as far as the Pacific seaboard to feed the demand, which at times reached more than a thousand horses a day. The tortuous process of acquiring the horses, sending them by rail car to the East Coast, where up to 50,000 were being held at any one time, then procuring and fitting out the shipping to take them across the Atlantic, was a gargantuan feat of organization.

Buying the horses in the first place was demanding enough. The British vets made a laconic list of the devices used to try and deceive them:

Sponges are placed up nostrils to hide unsoundness of wind. Teeth are scientifically 'bishoped' to hide age. Ice is placed in the rectum to hide high temperatures. Various dopes are given to stimulate sick animals to temporary activity.

Further ruses tested the vigilant British officers:

Substitution will, of a certainty, occur in a proportion of cases. Animals which have been rejected once are disguised in various ways and constantly offered a second time at a different purchasing centre even hundreds of miles away. And every possible pressure is liable to be placed on veterinary officers to relax their standards of examination.

Despite their best efforts to acquire sound, healthy horses, the British soon discovered that 75 per cent of their purchases would arrive sick at the East Coast holding yards, usually suffering from what was known as 'shipping fever' but was normally pneumonia.

They knew that if the horses came from good healthy stock brought up on the open range they had a much better chance than if they came from what was described as a 'pampered' environment. A batch of great Percherons purchased in Sioux City, straight from the Idaho ranges, all arrived in good condition after a rail journey of nearly 3,000 miles. But it soon became apparent that it was often the rail journey itself which caused the sickness. One of the great depots was at Newport News in Rhode Island. One train arrived there after an eighteen-hour delay. Twenty-four mules were offloaded from one car and dropped dead almost as soon as they reached their pens. The vets became all too familiar with the symptoms of impending death in such animals: the pulse was practically imperceptible, the ears and lips were cold, the gums and lips blue and there was a livid colour in the eye. Death came quite suddenly from cardiac arrest, often while the animal was still standing up.

The British made great efforts to alleviate these problems by acquiring or building yards at intervals along the track where the horses could be offloaded to be fed and watered for at least five hours, but ideally twelve hours or more, before continuing their journey. However, it was often hard to persuade the American and Canadian railway operators to run their trains satisfactorily. As late as the spring of 1918, the system was so disorganized that journeys which should have taken thirty-six hours were taking eleven days – and thirty-six hours was the maximum time, the vets knew, which horses could travel without the majority of them succumbing to shipping fever. The fact was they would hardly eat or drink en route, even if hay and water were provided. And then there was the weather. In the first winter of the war, the ferocious icy conditions contributed to disastrous levels of loss, which reached up to 50 per cent in animals going to the coast and caused the War Office in London to send out new teams of vets to see what the problems were and how they could be addressed.

The new men soon reported that the rail cars themselves were unsuitable. They had mainly been used for cattle and were exposed to the weather. There existed what were known as 'palace cars', which were used to carry racehorses and other valuable stock. But there were nothing like enough of these, and the War Office jibbed at paying for more – an almost certainly false economy, as it turned out.

The holding yards turned out to be another huge problem, both on the way at places like St Louis and Chicago, but above all at the main holding depots in the East, for that was where the animals had to be held until they were fit enough to go on board ship – it was well established that it was futile to attempt to send unfit horses by sea.

The attrition rate in the holding yards could be alarming. In 1917, when 99,000 horses had been killed in the preparation for and support of the battles around Passchendaele, there was a desperate push to acquire replacements from across the Atlantic. Standards dropped. Nearly 900 horses died of pneumonia and other diseases in the American holding yards in December of that year alone, and 500 sick horses a week were being pulled out of the yards and sent to the veterinary hospitals.

The big stockyards of the Midwest had been initially blamed for spreading infection, but it was gradually understood that the key lay with the Remount service's own yards. Above all, the animals needed hard standing and a roof over their heads. Turning them out in muddy paddocks, in the name of fresh air and exercise, was the reverse of helpful.

Once the animals were on board ship, the process was remarkably successful. Despite storm and tempest, crowded conditions, a shortage of experienced personnel aboard the ships and enemy action, only one in a hundred of the horses failed to walk down the gangplanks and on to European docksides. More than 700,000 were delivered to their fate in the service of the British armies. Only eleven horse transport ships were sunk in the whole war with, as the clerks in the Admiralty scrupulously recorded, 5,589 animals on board.

But it was not just North America. South Africa, Australia, New Zealand, the remotest parts of the Empire and beyond, all were scoured for animals for the battlefronts. One evocative account of how the work was done came from the now almost forgotten figure of R. B. Cunninghame Graham.

Cunninghame Graham had been a Radical MP, was a close friend of Joseph Conrad, a supporter of Karl Marx, the author of a dozen books and one of the founders of the Scottish National Party – and long a hero of the left, since his beating and arrest during the great Irish demonstration of 1887 in Trafalgar Square. He had been defended in court by Herbert Asquith, the future Prime Minister, but was still sentenced to six weeks in Pentonville prison.

When the War broke out, he was already more than sixty years old. But he volunteered immediately to help with the task of finding war horses. For nearly twenty years, from the age of seventeen, he had lived in the

Robert Cunninghame Graham, English School. *(Private Collection/ Ken Welsh/ Bridgeman Images)*

wildest reaches of Uruguay and Argentina among the *gauchos* and the *estancias* of the South American interior. The books he wrote about his adventures were hugely popular, and he became the correspondent and then the friend of Theodore Roosevelt.

In November 1914 he left Liverpool aboard the Royal Mail Ship *Arlanza* for Montevideo, accompanied by three vets and four other officers. On arrival, Don Roberto, as he was known to his friends in South America, soon found himself in familiar territory. He wrote home:

Today, after having parted our horses, I am camped out under some *paraiso* trees and roasted some meat. All round me were hundreds of horses, in front *pampa*, and to the left the great woods stretching down to the River Uruguay, and in the distance Entre Rios. Like the old days, we ate the meat with our knives (I used the one I bought in Gualeguaychu in 1871) and then we lay down on our saddles and had a siesta. There was a little warm wind blowing, making pleasant music among the green tufts of pampas grass which grew along the *arroyo* in front of us.

But it was an idyll with a dark side. In his next letter he wrote:

Last night I and the *gauchos* drove some five hundred horses through the plains in high grass. It was a wonderful sight, but sad to think it was their last happy day on earth.

Cunninghame Graham had set up his headquarters at a place called Bopicua, near the town of Fray Bentos in Uruguay. The system was that the *gauchos* were invited to bring in any horse that they wished to sell. Each animal was examined by the veterinary officers. Selection was rigorous, for they had to be fit not only for war but also for the long sea journey to England. Although the Uruguayan horse was considered tough and remarkably free from disease, almost two thirds were rejected. The chosen animals were brought in front of Cunninghame Grahame, who directed them to be branded, either on the neck with the word 'Artilleria' or on the hip with the word 'Caballeria' – artillery or cavalry. Then their manes were cut off. Payment was invariably in cash.

Now the arduous journey began. Cunninghame Graham's consignments did not have the facilities available in North America. Conditions were gruelling. First the horses were entrained at Fray Bentos for an eighteen-hour journey by rail to Montevideo. There six ships had been chartered. As the official report put it:

> The general system of fitment on these ships left much to be desired. No exercise was possible, nor could the feet be reached; and it was only with much difficulty, and the carpenter's assistance, that animals could be removed from their stalls in case of need.

The voyage passed through the tropics and took more than three weeks. The report continued:

> The system of watering horses from buckets is apt to be perfunctorily carried out unless attendants are very conscientious – an infrequent attribute of the horse attendant on board ship – or are closely supervised. The watering of twenty or twenty-five horses by one man from a small bucket along very narrow and crowded gangways is apt to result in the animals going short of water as a rule rather than an exception. In consequence, loss of condition will certainly ensue.

In practice the situation was greatly alleviated by English emigrants to South America who were returning to join the colours and who could at least supervise the matelots.

In the space of three months, 2,232 horses were despatched on the ships to England. Cunninghame Graham described his last consignment thus:

> The horses came out of the corral like a string of wild geese, neighing and looking round. Slowly we rode towards the herd, sending on several well mounted men upon its flanks, and with precaution, for horses easily take fright upon the march and separate. We got them into motion on a well marked trail that led towards the gate of the *estancia*, our headquarters. At first they moved a little sullenly, and as if surprised. Then the contagion of motion that spreads so rapidly amongst animals on the march seemed to inspire them, and the whole herd broke into a light trot. That is the moment when a stampede may

Troops Embarking at Southampton, John Lavery. (*Imperial War Museum, London, UK*)

happen, and accordingly we pulled our horses to a walk, whilst the men riding on the flanks forged slowly to the front, ready for anything that might occur. Gradually the trot slowed down, and we saw, as it were, a sea of manes and tails in front of us, emerging from a cloud of dust from which shrill neighings and loud snortings rose. Still seven miles lay between us and our camping ground. As the horses finally passed the gate, we counted them in. When the last animal had passed and the great gate swung to, a young man rode to my side and, looking at the troop, said, 'Eat well. There is no grass like that of Bopicua where you go across the sea. The grass in Europe must all smell of blood.'

Cunninghame Grahame took ship for England accompanied by a little pony called Malacara, which he had bought from an old man on the promise that it would not go to war. Malacara was to live with its new owner for nearly twenty years before finding its final resting place on his farm in Surrey.

When the purchased horses arrived in England they were at first farmed out to horsemen and farmers in the south of England who had the land and the expertise to help them recover from the rigours of the voyage. They then had to be assessed for suitability for the various tasks the war demanded. It was thus that the artist George Denholm Armour, then living at Purton Stoke in Hampshire, was drawn into the war. He took on a few of the imported horses and with the help of his friend the Australian poet Will Ogilvie – an outstanding horseman – began preparing them for duty.

The success of this enterprise resulted in Armour shortly being drafted in to command a squadron at the Swaythling Remount Depot on the edge of Southampton which was being rapidly expanded. It turned out that most of his staff had been coalminers, with little more equestrian experience than using pit ponies in the depths of their collieries. But Armour became a great admirer of their fortitude and ability to acquire the necessary skills, which included 'ride and lead' with a horse on either side as they were taken to be entrained or shipped to France.

Armour was at Swaythling for two years before arranging his assignment to the Remount Service in Salonika on the Bulgarian front. Throughout the war he continued to provide drawings and cartoons for *Punch* and *Country Life*, depicting the ways and manners of the unending project to maintain the supply of horses and mules for the battlefields.

John Lavery's picture of troops and horses embarking in a camouflaged ship at Southampton docks illustrates one element in the immensely efficient system for getting horses to the Western Front. Southampton, of all the English Channel ports, became the great hub for transport to Boulogne and Le Havre. More than a dozen ships a day made the crossing. At the beginning of the war in August, the minutely planned operation to take the requisitioned horses to France swung into action. Eighty trains arrived in one day at Southampton. Less than a fortnight after the declaration of war, more than 9,000 horses had been delivered to the British Expeditionary Force.

When the ships arrived across the Channel, the horses and mules were again loaded on to trains to take them to within a few miles of the Front. The journey was so quick that it was often considered unnecessary even to unsaddle them. From the railheads the troops collected their new animals for the final journey to the combat areas.

This effort also required huge amounts of feed and forage to sustain the animals. Later in the War, this onerous supply chain became the subject of much debate as the cavalry particularly lay unemployed behind the lines, yet absorbed shipping and rail transport which many of the commanders felt could be much more usefully devoted to ammunition and arms.

The exigencies of the War produced exceptional advances in the care of horses in a military environment. The Army's horsemen were told:

> A rail journey profoundly excites and disturbs horses which are not accustomed to this mode of conveyance. The CO of nearly every mounted unit has observed this extraordinary tendency to sickness among remounts transferred to his unit from a distant station.

High temperatures and pneumonia frequently developed. Careful observation demonstrated that these horses were not infected but were suffering from stress, which could quite frequently be fatal. A policy emerged that no rail journey in France should be longer than 50 miles, and that there should be at least 21 days between journeys.

Shipboard transport continued to be challenging. By early 1916, the authorities felt confident enough to produce a fairly stern pamphlet: horses should be carried loose in pens of five or six, or up to ten, not in stalls; the pens should have a hay net for each horse, ready before they came on board ('the horse begins to nibble at his hay as soon as he arrives and in this way speedily acquires greater confidence in his surroundings'). But watering was always the chief problem. Even when – as was frequently not the case – the horses were watered four times a day, slack supervision often left them thirsty.

The War Office urged transport officers 'to make friendly acquaintance with the ship's engineer officers. A thoughtful man will always find possibilities for improvement of conditions.' Aboard the heavily crowded SS *Englishman*, sailing through the tropics in 1915, thoughtful men came up with the plan to make all the feed troughs watertight and leave them full of water overnight. Others devised canvas wind scoops to funnel fresh air in to the horse decks. The *Englishman* arrived with only minimal casualties. 'The successful conducting officer,' concluded the official guidance, 'must be a hygienist and disciplinarian, a good horse master rather than a skilled prescriber.'

Tropical conditions proved a great hazard to horses at sea. The Australians, coming through the Red Sea and the Suez Canal in 1915 to join the Palestine campaign, lost nearly a third of their horses on some ships during the monsoon season. The SS *Itinda* lost twenty-six horses in one day in the Red Sea, when the temperature reached 104° Fahrenheit. Out of 533 horses which left Australia, 161 died. Most of these were being carried in the lower deck where ventilation was poor.

The learning curve in the early months of the War was steep. After the depredations of the retreat from Mons, remounts were urgently sought from the depots where the horses had been commandeered in England. Too many arrived in France in what the professionals regarded as a lamentable state, often unshod and unclipped. They were tied to horse lines by flimsy halters which allowed them to bite each other severely and kick. The 5th Cavalry, battered though it was in the retreat, had to refuse more than half the horses which were sent up to it near Braisne.

Three months into the War, a shipload of 319 heavy draught horses came from Deptford, all but 80 of which were classified as sick. Six months on, the horses were still arriving in France after the short journey from England in a deplorable state. In February 1915 a vet at Boulogne admitted more than 1,000 of the 1,800 who arrived into hospital with pneumonia.

Cavalry Memorial in Hyde Park, Adrian Jones. (Roy Fox)

Chapter 2

Cavalry

Captain Adrian Jones' mythic memorial of St George and the slain dragon in Hyde Park in London, erected, as it proclaims, by the Cavalry of the Empire to their fallen comrades, honours the final glory of the horseman in the war of 1914–18. Round the base are the bronze riders with turban, helmet, cap and cockade, and with lance, sabre and sword. Behind are the names of the great cavalry regiments: the Life Guards, Hussars and Scots Greys from Britain, but also the legendary detachments from India, Skinner's Horse, the Gwalior and Hyderabad Lancers and the Ratlam Despatch Riders.

The Imperial roll call goes on: the Aden Troop, the Otago Mounted Rifles from New Zealand, the East African Mounted Rifles, Lord Strathcona's Horse and the Fort Garrys from Canada; then all the British county regiments, from the Fife and Forfar to the Royal North Devon. Their war was madcap glory in Mesopotamia, desert endurance in Gaza and Jordan and endless frustration and footslogging sacrifice on the Western Front.

The cavalry in the Great War have suffered from the amnesia of hindsight. The books, the poetry, the films have all contributed to the notion that the cavalry were pampered elegants, glittering languidly behind the lines and contributing little but a drain on the brandy stores. Even in the forgotten war in Mesopotamia, T. E. Lawrence and his camels have eclipsed all memory of the cavalry's role in the defeat of the Turks.

Yet it is arguable that the cavalry saved the Allies at the beginning of the war in France, turned the enemy at the crucial moment in the great German breakthrough of March 1918 and with the intensely courageous charges at Beersheba and Romani in Palestine ended all prospects of Turkish victory in the Middle East.

In the first month of the war, August 1914, the Germans swept through Belgium and northern France, forcing open a gap between the French and British Armies which the German high command thought promised the swift and overwhelming victory for which they had planned.

The shadow of the aeroplane and the automobile had already been looming over the horses and the cavalry of Great Britain in the years before the outbreak of war. One airman staring out of his cockpit could claim to see as much as a whole troop of scouting horsemen. The armouring of cars – even the first sketch of tanks – was already on the drawing board. The fearsome effectiveness of machine guns, artillery and rifles made the flesh and blood of horse and man seem absurdly vulnerable. Yet in the first months of war it was the cavalry which proved the most crucial arm in first intercepting the German forces, then leading the controlled retreat from Mons, then effecting the rolling-up of the German retreat after the Battle of the Marne.

It was a cavalryman, Captain Charles Hornby of the 4th Dragoon Guards, who killed the first German to die at the hands of a British soldier in the war. This was an encounter of medieval simplicity. Early in the morning of 22 August, the Dragoons were edging their way forward at the very head of the British forces when they caught a glimpse of horsemen, glinting in their cuirassier equipment and armed with lances, making their way down a road ahead near the village of Casteau.

Hornby and his troop set off at the gallop and hurtled into the enemy in the main street of the village. Hornby, in the lead, drove his sword into a Cuirassier's chest, inflicting what was officially recognized as the first killing of the war. In the confines of the village street the Cuirassiers were finding it difficult to use their lances, designed as they were for the fields of nineteenth century Waterloo, rather than twentieth century semi-urban Belgium. The Dragoons accounted for a dozen or more and sent them packing.

An hour or so later, the 16th Lancers came across some German soldiers in a field full of corn. The discomfited Jägers tried to take cover behind the stooks, but to little effect, for this was textbook tilting-ring stuff for the Lancers. 'We speared quite a number on the way through,' recorded one Lancer, 'and then some more on the way back.'

As soon as the retreat from Mons began, it was again the cavalry who were summoned to save the day: lance and sword against rifle and machine gun, with Captain Francis Grenfell of the 9th Lancers winning the War's first Victoria Cross. The cavalry shepherded the British Expeditionary Force all the way back until the first turning point of the War at Néry. There again there took place an encounter of improbable pageantry. A trumpet major sounded the charge, the weapons were sword, sabre and lance, and 1,500 British horsemen sent 5,000 German cavalry fleeing.

One of the crucial moments in what became known as the Battle of the Marne was a cavalry action at Moncel, where the German cavalry were on the point of breaking through in early September. It is a classic tale of derring-do. The commander of the 9th Queen's Royal Lancers was Lieutenant David Campbell, a figure of improbable glamour and heroism who was to survive the war and end up as Colonel of his regiment. Campbell had already, as a young officer, won the Grand National on a horse he had bought and broken himself called The Soarer. He had nearly come down at Becher's Brook and then seen off the remainder of the field of twenty-eight by a length and a half up the Aintree run in. He then went on to win the Grand Military steeplechase and lead his team to win the Army polo championship, all in the same year.

At Moncel, Campbell, reconnoitring in front of his troops, suddenly bumped into a hundred or more German dragoons just mounting and ready for action. He made haste back to his men, who were behind a large haystack, resting after a day of bruising encounters. 'Being very well mounted,' as he put it, he had no difficulty in leaving them half a mile behind. His account goes on:

I brought the troop out from behind the haystack and gave the order Left Wheel Into Line Gallop. I forgot that I was riding a fresh horse and that the men's horses must be very tired, and did not perceive until I was about 100 yards from the German lines that I was about 100 yards ahead. It was, however, too late to wait, so I rode straight on, hoping for the best. As I approached the Germans, they closed in on their troop leader, and their long iron lances presented a very disagreeable looking wall. I directed my horse toward the troop leader, and when I got level with him I shot him as he was in the act of cutting at me with his sword. The next thing I remember was being carried very slowly over the tail of my horse to fall in a sainfoin field. Both the Germans and our own men passed right over the top of me, but, marvellous to relate, not a single horse trod on my body. I got up on to my knees and saw the German cavalry galloping away in the utmost confusion.

Moncel was about as far as the Germans got, before their withdrawal which ended in the long 'stabilization' of the trenches.

The 9th Lancers went on to be involved in a number of mounted actions, and the British cavalry covering the retreat of the British Expeditionary Force had a series of encounters with the Uhlans, the classically helmeted and armed German cavalry. In early September, there occurred the last recorded occasion when cavalry charged at each other lance to lance. One witness described his first sight of the Germans:

Magnificent in the morning sun they rode, a solid line rising and falling with regular cadences as though mechanically propelled, the finest of the German Army were charging across the fields.

It was the Germans' misfortune, however, to meet the finest cavalry in the British Army, the 9th Lancers. Their commanding officer gathered his troop with their lances at the ready, quietly said, 'Follow me, Gentlemen,' and led a galloping charge against the oncoming Germans. The sheer dash and speed of the Lancers proved decisive. There was a clash of steel and the Lancers rode right through the German line. A number of the Germans were speared right through. 'Look there is blood on my hand, ' one of the Lancers said to his commanding officer, as he tried to extract his lance from a German. The remaining Germans galloped away.

Sadly, Flanders to this day contains a roll call of names synonymous with slaughter: Ypres, the Somme, Passchendaele, Arras. But there remains too the echo of charnel places where the horses suffered: Monchy, where a squadron of the 10th Hussars lost every single one of their horses – they and the Essex Yeomanry lost nearly a thousand horses all told.

Then there is Néry, where the Bays, the Royal Horse Artillery and the 5th Dragoons lost more than 350 horses in one action early in the war; and Audregnies, where the cavalry charged over three quarters of a mile of open ground against well entrenched German guns and lost 169 men and more than 300 horses.

Captain Francis Grenfell at Audregnies, Richard Caton Woodville. (*National Army Museum, London, UK*)

Woodville's painting of the rescue of the guns records the incident at Audregnies when Captain Francis Grenfell of the 9th Lancers won the first Victoria Cross of the War, only a week after the British Expeditionary Force had arrived in August 1914. The knee-to-knee cavalry charge had ended with the survivors milling about chaotically in front of wire 'like rabbits being driven in front of guns' as Grenfell later described it. Then came the traditional job of the cavalry in retreat – much called upon in the Boer War a decade earlier – of trying to save the guns. Mostly dismounted, the Lancers did indeed get the artillery out. Grenfell, wounded, became a national hero, with the King coming to see him in hospital. Indeed, Audregnies, for all its forlorn failure to stop the German advance, produced many extraordinary stories which captivated the Press in those first weeks of fighting, including that of a Dragoon officer and a bandsman who, wounded and captured, escaped from hospital and walked for several days through the German lines in the dark, reached the coast and took ship to England.

Both Sir John French and Douglas Haig, the British commanders in France, resisted the many attempts to diminish or even abolish the mounted Yeomanry and Cavalry regiments. Haig, in particular, believed that the cavalry were the only available means of rapidly following up any major breakthrough achieved by the assault of infantry and artillery. The Germans did, effectively, as the trench war became prolonged, eliminate their cavalry. There are strategists who still maintain that when the Germans' chance to force the supreme victory came with their almost overwhelming attack of March 1918, the lack of cavalry was the crucial factor in Hindenburg's inability to follow up his initial successes.

The cavalry were moved about incessantly in the rear areas of the Western Front, as one requirement or another demanded their presence. But that did not deter them from reproducing to the maximum the ordered, structured and haughty efficiency which they cherished at home. As soon as a movement order appeared, the advance party was despatched to find the most appealing chateau or other residence for the officers. The NCOs then identified the local houses on which they could impose themselves, and particularly the farms with buildings which could accommodate a troop of horses. The daily routine – hours of brushing and strapping in the morning and then again in the evening, morning exercise, weapons practice – prevailed as vigorously as on any common day at Horse Guards.

During the four years following the battles in the early months of the war, there were still to be times when the classic cavalry role was required in limited actions. But the mounted soldiers soon found that they were doomed to occupy many of the least glamorous roles in the Army. Cavalrymen became the clean-up brigade after German trenches had been taken, the bringers-out of the dead and the wounded, the makers of roads through the mud and the slime, the carriers of ammunition and supplies and the guardians of the communication cables.

Nor was it long before the men, dismounted, were expected to do their stints in the front line trenches. For many this began with a posting to the infamous Bull Ring training establishment at Etaples. There the conditions were so bad that in September 1917 they provoked the only large-scale mutiny which the British Army suffered in the entire war. The trainees had been forced through gas-filled tunnels to test their equipment, then thrown into the most exhausting of assault courses and incessantly bullied by the instructors, as well as being subjected to field punishments such as being tied to the wheels of guns for whole days, with floggings and imprisonment for those who failed to stay the course.

For the horses of the Yeomanry and cavalry, too, there were tribulations for which no training had prepared them. In the winter mud they became so cold that it took days for them to recover. Frequently, horses stuck in the mud could not be freed and had to be shot. Hay and forage was rationed to barely subsistence level.

But despite these debilitating trials, the cavalry were called upon to make regular interventions, even in the midst of some of the great battles of the War.

During the battle of the Somme in July 1916, the 7th Dragoon Guards and the Indian Secunderabad Brigade were summoned to a part of the line near Longueval where the German defences had been broken. They made their way past cheering British troops, agog at the sight of immaculate mounted men armed with lances and sabres, picking their way through the shattered landscape and the unburied bodies. Led by Lieutenant Pope of the Dragoons, they proceeded along a shallow valley until suddenly they encountered German machine gunners. Pope immediately turned his lancers and charged up the slope. Fifteen Germans were fatally speared and another thirty-two surrendered. Further German resistance stalled the advance, but Pope then rode out and successively retrieved three of his wounded men, slinging them across his saddle to bring them back.

In the opening weeks of the war, when the Germans pushed to within 25 miles of Paris, were then stopped on the River Marne, turned west and then were themselves pushed back 60 miles to the River Aisne, the cavalry on both sides were in constant action.

The halting of the German advance to the Marne can credibly be attributed to another cavalry action at the village of Néry. Lieutenant Norrie told how a squadron of the 11th Hussars 'charged with a rousing cheer and drawn swords. The enemy surrendered, shouting "Kamerad, Kamerad".' The Hussars captured eight guns and two machine guns. From this point, the Allied advance back towards the River Aisne commenced.

A recurring refrain throughout the War was to be the search for 'The Gap', or 'the big G', through which the cavalry could hurtle and go on to conclusive victory. Gaps did appear, even during the years of trench warfare, but were universally either missed or unexploited. In the first three weeks of the War, the German cavalry, which was present with thousands of horses, failed to take advantage of numerous gaps which opened up between the French and British forces. Once the tide turned, the British cavalry, too, missed a number of opportunities.

Even close up to the Front, mounted officers were a common sight. But, apart from the cavalry actions late in the War, few men expected to see horses deployed in a major attack. Yet when the fog lifted on the morning of the great Kaiser's battle on 21 March 1918, British troops were astonished to see an equestrian panorama moving across no-man's-land towards them. There were cavalry, horse-drawn wagons, mounted infantry officers, horse ambulances.

All, it would appear, in expectation of a painless German victory after their great artillery barrage. But the British Lewis machine guns opened up and, as a British soldier recalled, soon there was nothing moving except for riderless horses: 'We could hear the shrieks of stricken horses, but they eventually galloped away.'

The Canadian cavalry – the Fort Garrys and Strathcona's Horse – and Alfred Munnings serendipitously encountered each other at the beginning of 1918. In a matter of only eight weeks the artist created the paintings which are an enduring record of the most intense and demanding cavalry action and a unique record of the life of a brigade who had been in France almost throughout the War. While Munnings was with them, the Canadians were to be at the sharpest point of the German March offensive, and then to be called upon to make perhaps the most decisive cavalry charge of the entire war.

The first painting Munnings made on his arrival in France was of the Canadian cavalry's commander Jack Seely on his horse Warrior. Seely, a Boer War veteran who had been a British Cabinet Minister, had been appointed to lead the Canadian cavalry when they first arrived in England. Soon after Seely took command, the brigade embarked at Southampton and arrived in Boulogne on 3 May. The brigade had brought 1800 horses from Canada. But in less than three weeks they found themselves, horseless, sent to fight in the trenches at Festubert near Ypres. For seven months they suffered the relentless trials of mud and machine guns and casualties which were the lot of the infantry in Flanders. They lost a quarter of their men within the first week.

But the British commanders still believed that the day of the cavalry would come. And as the thinking and the preparations for the great offensives of 1916 matured, the Canadians came out of the trenches and were restored to their horses. When the Somme attack came at the beginning of July, the Strathconas and the Fort Garrys were close up behind the line, armed with detailed orders and maps of where they were to go to sweep up the fleeing Germans after the artillery and infantry had carved the necessary gap in the German line.

They waited in vain. But the task of exploiting 'The Gap' was regularly assigned to the cavalry, and later the new tanks, before every attack for the next two years.

Throughout 1916 and 1917 there were episodes of brief but classic cavalry action. Lieutenant Fred Harvey of Strathcona's won the brigade's first Victoria Cross leading an attack on the German-held hilltop village of Guyencourt. He rode directly at the German machine gunners, was knocked off his horse, but still managed to destroy the enemy on foot with his revolver.

At the end of 1917, the Canadians were part of more than 25,000 cavalry lined up behind the infantry at Cambrai, primed again to exploit The Gap. Again, it never came, though there was a series of engagements, when the Strathconas captured some German guns and some prisoners.

By the time Munnings arrived in February 1918 the Canadians were battle hardened but yet to achieve what would be the most heroic feats of their war. Munnings soon won the cooperation of the soldiers, and rapidly produced the most evocative paintings.

Halt on the March by a Stream at Nesle is an almost bucolic scene. For it was indeed a very warm March in 1918. The troopers have got the saddles off many of the horses and are relaxing themselves. The horses are settling into their nosebags. Despite the press of horses, there is an air of calm and confidence. *Strathcona's Horse on the March*, the horses clipped and shining, shows the full equipment which the cavalry horse had to carry. Weapons, feed, water, the trooper himself, often meant the horse was carrying 300lb.

The artists were welcomed with total civility by the troops. Even during the debilitating retreat to the Avre, Munnings, improbably attired in odd items of different uniforms, describes the billet that General Seely found for him in the Vicomte Villeneuve's family chateau at Davenescourt on the Somme. Dinner was provided while the regimental band played in the main hall. Upstairs, William Orpen was painting Seely's portrait, having just finished one of the grand French Marshal Foch, while Munnings was painting Prince Antoine of Orleans on a black horse.

Seely took Munnings up to the great master bedroom with the comment 'This is my Ecole des Beaux Arts'. All this, as the German advance progressed inexorably. Within days the chateau was overrun, its contents entirely destroyed, and its proprietor a refugee. After the war Munnings discovered to his astonishment that among the few items the Vicomte had taken with him was Munnings' portrait of the Prince, which thus survived.

Munnings also spent some time with the Canadian foresters who had come to France to help with the vital supply of timber to the trenches and sketched a pair of lumber horses, Percheron types, at a mill in the Forest of Dreux.

Encouraged – indeed, driven – by Lord Beaverbrook, the Canadian government commissioned more than a dozen artists to go to the Western Front, including Lieutenant Alfred Bastien, in fact a Belgian painter with an already considerable reputation before he was recruited to join the Canadians in France in 1918. His picture of Canadian cavalry waiting in a wood has an unreal, timeless quality. This sylvan hideaway seems impossibly distant from the world of artillery, shell holes, trenches and devastated landscape usually associated with the war in Flanders. But it was essential in all cavalry tactics to seek maximum cover, valleys, dips in terrain, buildings, before launching a charge. The accounts of cavalry actions throughout the four years in France invariably emphasize the use of haystacks, woodland, abandoned buildings, riverbeds, to infiltrate the horsemen as close as possible to the enemy before the charge.

By contrast, Bastien's painting of cavalry and tanks advancing towards Arras in the final push of 1918 is a vista of shattered hazards and obstructions over devastated ground. It is a reminder that when tanks first appeared in the Great War they were regarded as a fortified addition to the cavalry, designed to augment rather than displace the mounted arm.

One cavalry horse, however, blessed with a supernaturally charmed life and a most distinguished owner, survived the war to become as famous in England in the 1920s as Sefton, the Household Cavalry survivor of an IRA nail bomb, became in the 1970s. Warrior

Halt by a Stream, Sir Alfred Munnings. (© *Canadian War Museum, Ottawa, Canada*)

Strathcona's March, Sir Alfred Munnings. (© *Canadian War Museum, Ottawa, Canada*)

Cavalry and Tanks at Arras, Alfred Bastien. (© *Canadian War Museum, Ottawa, Canada*)

Canadian Cavalry Ready in a Wood, Alfred Bastien. (© Canadian War Museum, Ottawa, Canada)

belonged to Jack Seely, Lord Mottistone, and his tale was told in a book written by his owner in 1924.

Seely, who had been Secretary of War in 1913 alongside Winston Churchill at the Admiralty, went to France with some of the earliest units at the outbreak of war in August 1914. Warrior went with him. Almost immediately, in the chaotic initial retreat before the German assault, Seely found himself lending Warrior to the BEF commander, Sir John French. It was Warrior that the General rode as he steadied the British divisions in the first Battle of Ypres.

Seely's book gives an extraordinary portrait of his horse's time in France. There was a week's furlough behind the lines at an airfield, where much entertainment was had from laying bets on Warrior racing an aircraft as it took off. Seely tells us that the station commander fixed the winning line so that there was often a dead heat. Then, Seely tells us:

At intervals in the lull of battle we would have sports, including horse shows. Warrior and I used to put up some sort of a show when we happened to be out of the line, but when my great friend Geoffrey Brooke rode him, Warrior became the star turn, and won every prize for good looks, for jumping, and for docility.

Yet the main business was, of course, the battlefield. The horses were as much a target as the troops. Seely describes Warrior's many escapes:

On one occasion when Warrior was stuck fast in the mud on the Somme, a German flew down and emptied his machine gun belt at us; the bullets were very near, but not one of them hit us. Once a great shell fell near him, and he was completely buried under the falling earth, except for one forefoot. But with the help of a little digging we got him out unharmed, except for a lameness in the off fore which has troubled him from time to time ever since.

Warrior carried Seely through many encounters, including the mounted attack on Guyencourt when the Germans were withdrawing from the Somme. This was the battle when the Canadian Captain Harvey of Strathcona's Horse gained the only Victoria Cross earned in mounted action on the Western Front.

The evening of that same day, Seely rode forward and, he says, beheld a strange spectacle, perhaps unique in all those four years of fighting:

A mile and a quarter eastward, in the sunlight of this bright winter's evening, I saw three squadrons of German cavalry facing us. How well I remember that moment sitting astride my Warrior, rejoicing at having seen one of my men do a deed of valour that would live for ever, and looking over the flat plain at the German cavalry drawn up in battle array. Warrior had seen the German horses. He neighed loudly and tried to go forward. I said to my ADC, 'Warrior is right. Let's charge into the middle of them.'

Seely on Warrior, Sir Alfred Munnings. (© *Canadian War Museum, Ottawa, Canada*)

Wiser counsels prevailed. But it was as close to a true clash of cavalry as the Western Front ever offered.

Warrior's finest hour was to come during the final great German assault of March 1918. The Germans, having done a deal with Lenin to halt the war on the Eastern Front, had thrown all their resources into the great spring offensive. Their objective was the Channel ports. The British Army would be cut off and denied supplies. The Germans saw it as the chance for a killer blow before American troops could arrive in the early summer. The attack was dauntingly effective and by the end of March had come within sight of Amiens – and thus a breakthrough. The key point was the Moreuil Ridge, which overlooked Amiens. The Germans occupied it on 28 March.

The Allies had been pushed into a desperate sequence of retreat, then an attempt to hold ground, then further retreat. Seely, with his small brigade of horse, found himself at Moreuil village, held for the moment by some French soldiers.

It seemed to me quite clear that unless we recaptured the Moreuil Ridge, it was all over with Amiens, and probably with the Allied cause … Sitting there on Warrior's back I decided to attempt the apparently impossible … Warrior was strangely excited; all trace of exhaustion had gone; he pawed the ground with impatience. In some strange way, without the least doubt, he knew that the crisis in his life had come.

Seely's plan was to gallop through the front line of defending French infantry and up the hill to the wooded ridge from which German infantry and machine gunners were dominating the field. He paused to tell his comrades that the faster they galloped the more certain they were of success.

I could hardly finish my sentence before Warrior took charge. With a great leap he started off. All sensation of fear had vanished from him as he galloped on at racing speed. There was of course a hail of bullets from the enemy as we mounted the hill, but Warrior cared for nothing. His one idea was to get at the enemy. He almost buried his head in the brushwood when we reached the point of the wood. We were greeted by twenty or thirty Germans, who fired a few shots before running, doubtless thinking there were thousands of us following. It was a wonderful day. The main attack and Flowerdew swept up, and the wood was soon filled with galloping Canadian horsemen.

Eventually all German resistance on the ridge was overcome. Seely later wrote:

I must record, and it is indeed the truth, that so far as I am concerned, the credit for this wild adventure, which succeeded in so miraculous a fashion, was due not to me, but to my horse Warrior. He it was who did not hesitate and did not flinch, though well he knew the danger of those swift bullets which he had seen kill so many hundreds of men and horses all around him in the preceding years.

Writing years later, Seely remained convinced that his horse Warrior had saved not only the day but conceivably the whole Allied cause in that courageous charge to the top of the Moreuil Ridge.

Warrior survived the last months of the war to return home to Seely's house on the Isle of Wight – still fit enough to win the local point to point in 1921.

Chapter 3

Guns and Artillery

The gun horses, the Army vets thought, had the most demanding task of all. They had to carry almost the same weight as a cavalry horse in equipment and supplies, yet at the same time help to haul an artillery piece weighing a ton and a half or more through the most demanding terrain.

In the desert campaigns the vets became so concerned at the attrition of artillery horses that they instituted a regime of post mortem examination. They found many of the animals with enlarged hearts, which they attributed to the extreme severity of the work they were required to do. In France and Flanders too, from 1916, there were more than 100,000 artillery horses and mules among the half million animals in service, facing as testing conditions as any in the desert.

Yet the role of the gun horse has vanished from history. The most authoritative recent history of the artillery in the Great War devotes more than two hundred pages of erudite analysis to the evolution of guns, ammunition and strategy, but with virtually no mention of the animals who battled unremittingly to drag the weaponry to its appointed spot.

The Royal Artillery has no records of the thousands of horses who hauled the guns in the Great War. The animals were regarded by the regiment as tools – as they were lost or destroyed, new ones were simply drawn from stores.

Fortunately, the war artists were to leave a record of the challenges and intensity of the gun horses' work in a series of dramatic and expansive paintings.

Forward the Guns, Lucy Kemp-Welch's vast panorama of the Royal Horse Artillery hurtling out of the canvas at full pelt, impresses the might of the gun horses on the imagination beyond any words. It was the most lauded work at the Royal Academy exhibition of 1917.

Kemp-Welch was already a renowned animal painter before the war began. She was still in her twenties when her picture *Colt Hunting in the New Forest* was bought for the Tate Gallery. Early in the War she was commissioned by a parliamentary committee to produce a recruiting picture. She was unable, because of a leg injury, to go to France with the Red Cross, but was thus available to work in 1916 on *Forward the Guns* at the artillery base at Bulford on Salisbury Plain.

Here she had the enthusiastic help of the commanding officer, Colonel Yorke – a 'treasure', as she described him. The colonel organized his troops to gallop right up as close as they dared to the artist, and then to repeat the manoeuvre several times. After that she spent many days painting the uniforms, the insignia and the individual horses, to produce a work which enshrines for ever the dash, bravery and discipline of the gun horses of the Great War.

Artillery on Flanders Dunes, Adrian Jones. (*National Army Museum, London, UK*)

Horse-drawn Transports Passing the Ruined Cloth Hall, Ypres, Gilbert Holiday. (*National Army Museum, London, UK*)

Forward the Guns!, Lucy Kemp-Welch. (Tate Images, London, UK)

When, after the War, Lieutenant Ernest Millard saw Gilbert Holiday's painting of the ruined Cloth Hall at Ypres – the gun horses making their way with solitary purpose across the flattened devastation of the town – he realized he was seeing himself. He recalled:

In October 1917, the big attack was on and my groom and I were leading the horses through the town and towards the Front, and I noticed an artist painting. I never thought I would actually see myself in the finished work.

Millard had joined the Royal Horse Artillery in 1916 after leaving his apprenticeship in the family printing firm, having been in the Officer Training Corps at Lancing College. He recounts how – unlike in the cavalry – almost none of the officer cadets could ride. At the barracks in St John's Wood in London, the first lesson every day was designed to instil the basics of horse riding: 'Captain Hans would shout "Jump that jump" and if you fell off you just had to do it again.' Soon the cadets were confident enough to be racing their chargers across Regent's Park. Then they were put into the gun teams – six horses pulling the 13-pounder guns, with all the subtleties of managing the outer wheeler horses and the leaders and middles – in more dashing manoeuvres back in the Park.

Millard went via the Royal School of Artillery at Larkhill to France, where he realized that at the Front the horses were all-important to the Artillery and were treated with maximum care and affection. 'I have seen men cry,' he recalled, 'when their horses were killed or wounded.' During the retreat of March 1918 the horses were crucial in recovering the guns. The teams were kept behind the gun pits, but then had to be brought forward and limbered up to the guns to drag them out. 'I have seen us having to do this,' he said, 'within a hundred yards of the Germans.'

There were fierce disagreements about how to manage the gun horses in the dreadful conditions in France. Hervey de Montmorency, an artillery officer, disdainfully accused the Veterinary Officers of:

living in perpetual terror of mange. If one horse so much as twitched his skin, every animal in the district would be clipped closely from mane to tail. In depriving the wretched beasts of their warm coats, they slew thousands of them with pneumonia.

De Montmorency insisted that his horses were clipped only under the throat and chest. Their legs, too, were left untouched. He had his horses fed, rather unorthodoxly, on oats soaked in hot water. In the winter of 1917 he noted with mournful satisfaction that his horses stood the fierce weather much better than any of the others.

De Montmorency recorded the ordeal of life in the Ypres Salient. The teams were tethered to their lines in open fields in full view of the German captive balloons. They were exposed to artillery fire by day and bombs from aeroplanes overnight – something which de Montmorency, who had fought in the Boer War, found uniquely terrifying. His brigade lost

During a Battle (Field Guns), William Roberts. *(Imperial war Museum, London, UK)*

seven hundred horses in six weeks from these unceasing bombardments. His drivers used to have to lead pack horses loaded with cans of water along the duckboard tracks under cover of darkness to the front lines. 'Those poor beasts,' he wrote, 'which slipped or stumbled off these narrow causeways were often drowned in the liquid mud, or died of exhaustion after struggling for hours in a quicksand.' The heavy horses were required to haul guns and heavy loads of ammunition for 20 miles and back on a feed ration of 8lb of corn – compared with 10lb or 12lb a day at home. 'The horses suffered terribly,' he said, 'dying like flies.'

British officers, who admired the science, the efficiency and indeed the courage of the French Army, were nevertheless almost universally critical of French horse management. The French cavalryman almost never dismounted to rest his horse. Hay was regarded as the mainstay diet, with little corn or hard food. Precious little effort was put in to providing shelter, even in the worst weather.

The geography of the Ypres Salient can be easily comprehended today from the small country roads which loop round to the north of the restored town. Stop just two or three miles out of the town, and you can see an unimpressive ridge of ground towards the horizon. That is Passchendaele. Only a mile or two to the left are some new apartments, and the same to the right. Within this arc a million men were killed or wounded in four years, during which the front line hardly moved. It is quite easy to see still why Passchendaele really mattered. From that ridge the Germans could sometimes even see the sea and Allied ships. Every day they could look down on the Allied trenches. They had fixed balloons which carried cameras and lenses to record patterns of movements. And every day and night the Germans knew their opponents had to re-supply the men in the forward trenches.

Much of the latter work was done by horses. The Allies built elaborate screens to try and hide the columns of horses carrying ammunition, water and food from the sight of the enemy gunners. The horse routes snaked and zigzagged over rough duckboards towards the front. The legendary Flanders mud meant that if a laden horse fell off the narrow route it could often not be recovered. They had no cover in the horse lines, winter or summer. Like the town of Ypres itself, literally every building in the Salient had been flattened by shell fire. Yet the horses had to be concentrated together in order for them to be fed and watered.

Screened and disguised as these horse lines were, they were far more exposed than the trenches, and consequently the shell fire could reap daunting havoc. Injured and wounded horses added to the panic and had to be caught and shot. Where survival and return to work seemed possible, they had to be led back to the veterinary camps along the serpentine routes which were being used for the human casualties.

Thousands of horses were, inevitably, wounded by shell fire and bullets. Every effort of surgery and care went into trying to save them, often right behind the lines. The official history remarked, 'It is astonishing how much good work can be done with the aid of a scalpel and dressing forceps, a few pairs of artery forceps, a razor, scissors, and a needle and silk.'

Lieutenant Wylie of the Army Veterinary Corps recorded with professional detachment a typical incident.

> We were sheltering from aeroplane vision by the side of a wood when a German shrapnel shell burst on percussion among the trees, killing four horses outright and wounding ten others, two of these so severely that I shot them immediately. Of the others, one had a bullet wound on the near side of the neck. It passed through to the other side as far as the skin and then became deflected downwards over the shoulder and along the thorax, leaving its course clearly demonstrated like the weal produced by the crack of a whip. I traced this with my hand as far as the fourteenth or fifteenth rib where I could distinctly feel the bullet rolling about subcutaneously. From this situation, I removed it with a scalpel quite readily.

The horse duly recovered.

Most of the operations were helped by using chloroform. Older vets noted sardonically that young vets were able to get plenty of practice in 'without the fear of losing a client or having to pay for a patient'. Practice included removing the ovaries of difficult mares, and castrations.

The endless mud of Flanders meant the constant appearance of gravelled or 'quitter' feet, which usually required some form of farriery or surgery. But it was man-made foot problems which agitated the vets most. Ammunition boxes were nailed together, and soldiers opening them were scarcely likely to concern themselves too much with where the nails went. But so many horses suffered from nails in their feet that a concerted campaign was launched to try and make the soldiers more solicitous of the horses' welfare, including litter boxes with a notice saying, 'Please Put Nails in Here'.

In the later days of the war, as the Allies were moving forward, a villainous new German device appeared. One vet wrote:

> Terrible injuries were inflicted by the brutal caltrops, or crow's feet [small four-pointed metal contrivances], thousands of which were thrown down by the Germans in the muddy tracks over which they knew our horses must follow in pursuit. The weight of the horse treading on these would cause the point to penetrate through the hoof, and sometimes right into the bone, fracturing it and often penetrating the navicular joint.

Research back home at Durham University produced, by 1917, a new medication of bismuth and iodoform. Used as a paste on open wounds, it 'saved many patients'. In Salonika the vets tried with considerable success simply applying petrol to wounds to defeat infection.

From time to time there were clusters of problems. An affliction of the groin and urinary tract called paraphimosis appeared in great numbers of animals in 1917. The vets reported:

Horse Lines, John Singer Sargent. (*Imperial War Museum, London, UK*)

The horses had passed through an exceptionally terrible time of hardship and exposure, being worked to the utmost because of a big advance and not being allowed extra food on account of the impossibility of transporting it to them. The weather too was exceptionally severe, and the mud conditions were appalling. Many arrived at the reception hospital in an emaciated condition. Numbers died in the trucks, and others fell down paralysed in the hind quarters and were shot at the station. Some were too far gone to obtain relief.

But quite a number, with simple surgery, were saved.

Chapter 4

The Somme and the Western Front

Will Dyson in 1916 was the first Australian to be appointed an official war artist. He wasted no time in getting as close as possible to the fighting then erupting on the Somme. He made numerous drawings, but this picture of three grooms on horseback at Franvillers behind the Somme – notably smart and relaxed – is a reminder that even close to the Front many regimental officers still had their chargers with them and Army grooms to look after them.

At a crucial phase of the Battle of the Somme, on September 15, the Coldstream Guards found themselves halted near the village of Ginchy by heavy losses from rifle and machine gun fire. They were famously rallied by Lieutenant Colonel John Vaughan Campbell, for many years Master of the Tamar Valley Harriers. Appearing on his charger at the Coldstreams' third line, he took out his hunting horn and summoned an advance. The guardsmen followed him and reached that day's objective. Lionel Edwards' drawing shows him in the mid-distance standing in the stirrups and flourishing the horn.

Campbell was awarded the VC for this legendary exploit. No mention was made of his horse in the official *London Gazette* citation, but he gave a personal account of the action to Edwards, so we must assume that the drawing's accuracy enjoyed Campbell's endorsement.

As soon as war had been declared, there was an instant impulse in many men to 'do their bit'. Among the first to organize were the British Royal Automobile Club. Their members, car owners, immediately offered to provide their cars and drivers to transport senior officers in France. This became the formal RAC Corps. One of the first to join and go overseas was an American living in London, Frederic Coleman.

He was allocated to the British First Cavalry Division. The work kept Coleman moving around behind and even close up to the Front, so that he saw much more than most soldiers. He kept a diary, which he published in the second year of the war to contribute to the campaign to persuade the United States to come in and join the Allies.

He described a trip near Chavonne to take Colonel Hamilton-Grace to report to the commander, Haig, and seeing a German aircraft drop a signal uncomfortably close, to direct German shellfire:

The road at that point was full of cavalry horses and ammunition wagons. Down went my foot on the accelerator pedal. The car leaped forward. I narrowly missed a horse. The shells came in. But we got into sight of Haig's headquarters. As we drew near, a wounded black mare, her side covered with mud, galloped madly past. A scared group of transport drivers were huddled behind a stone cairn by the roadside. We came to a dead horse in the road. Reaching Haig's chateau wall, we found the ditch piled full of dead horses and men. Two dismembered horses lay in the way, other dead horses were piled in the field. Fifteen horses and a dozen men was the toll taken by that one shell.

Two days later, Coleman described the gun horses at work during a German attack:

A battery commander was ordered to move his guns to another position. On the arrival of the gun horses the battery was heavily shelled. Back the horses were rushed under cover. Again they were ordered up and again the Germans started to shell them. After a wait of twenty minutes, the horses were brought up for the third time, only to be shelled and driven back as before.

Eventually, Coleman tells us, the British realized there had to be someone directing the fire. They searched the local village and discovered what Coleman calls 'a strapping chap in peasant garb' with binoculars. He was a German guardsman who had been left behind to spy for just such a purpose, and the horses were being brought up right under his eyes. 'To execute the spy and shift the battery was but a matter of moments,' Coleman notes.

One of the officers whom Coleman regularly chauffeured about was a cavalryman, Archibald Home, who had been at Sandhurst with Winston Churchill and was to survive the war with the rank of Brigadier-General and a knighthood. He went to France in 1914 with the first batch of cavalry in August. Home was to keep a meticulous and detailed diary of his war service. Within a matter of days, as he was being driven by Coleman in his big open-topped car, Home had something to record:

Had first personal brush with Uhlans [the German cavalry whom the British cavalry regarded as their proper opponents]. We were motoring towards Jouy-le-Cha when suddenly I saw three mounted German Lancers coming down the road about 300 yards away. I got hold of the rifle in the car. Jaco and I jumped out, and loosed off at them. They made off down the road. We did not hit one. It was rotten bad shooting on our part.

This incident happened on the first Sunday in September. But it was also Home's last glimpse of conventional cavalry action for almost the entire war. From then on, his diary is, in effect, a text for the view that has prevailed for so long, that the cavalry horses were an implausible adornment to the reality of the fighting on the Western Front. After the retreat from Mons, Home's cavalrymen were used for months on end as dismounted infantrymen in the trenches. Home describes the innumerable small pushes and retreats which characterized the Front throughout 1915. He is not only reconciled to their new duty but proud of their courage and morale in the trenches. In his diary he repeatedly expresses his hope that the Russians will be the means of bringing the war to an end with their attacks in the East. He remains sanguine that the pressure of German losses will bring peace, or better still the collapse of Germany.

Grooms on the Somme, William Dyson. (*Australian War Memorial, Canberra, Australia*)

Throughout the months and then years of the diary, Home, the cavalryman, scarcely mentions the horses, except to lament that in the wintry weather they are left standing in the open: 'They all have long coats, but they did not look too happy.'

When the cavalry went into the trenches, one man in every four was left behind to look after the horses. Home himself seemed to use his mare Mary Antoinette largely for recreation or local transport. After a year of war his diary records:

Got out for a long ride in the morning. It is a lovely country for riding over – now the crops are cut, one can gallop for miles. Very fine and hot. Saw a good many partridges.

In the spring:

Went to the 2ⁿᵈ Cavalry Division horse show. It was one of the best shows I have seen. Very well run and people collected from miles around. I saw a whole host of old friends.

By the summer, Home was beginning to have his doubts about the rectitude of this sort of thing.

Went to the Indian Cavalry Corps horse show. A wonderful sight – but was it war? I don't think so. It was a brave sight – but yet men were fighting not twenty miles away.

From time to time the cavalry were back in their saddles behind a planned British attack. But Home is sceptical in the extreme of the likelihood of their being used in the small gaps which might appear in the German lines. He is also dismissive of the French cavalry:

They are fine fellows the Frenchmen, but their training for war has been hopeless. They are armed with a popgun – a small carbine. I believe they would charge anything if you asked them to do so. But to see them trying to skirmish across a field is too funny for anything, only it is very serious as they are then wasted. Fine men too, the pick of the people.

There are occasional references from Home to the toll on horses. He mentions a military policeman sent out to cut saddles and harness off dead horses: 'He was promptly sick. But the natural remedy is to go out every day until he gets used to it.'

Home was to stay in France until the end of the war. He was aware of the Canadian cavalry's exploits ('They do it in their usual style – plenty of dash, but not much science'). But even in the last weeks of the war, with the advance towards Germany itself, Home felt his cavalrymen were being left behind, though suffering for all that:

Opposite: *Colonel Campbell with a Horn*, Lionel Edwards. (*Author*)

Wagon Lines, George Armour. (*Private Collection/Gorringes Auction Galleries*)

We have had many accidents lately through horses striking unexploded shells. Cyril Hankey's two horses were killed, and the groom lost a leg. It is a bad lookout for the future cultivators of the land.

John Glubb, who became famous as Glubb Pasha, commander of the Arab Legion during and after the Second World War, went to France at the age of eighteen as a Royal Engineers officer. He, too, kept a diary, which only emerged fifty years later, of life on the Western Front.

The diary paints a relentless picture of the hellish conditions in which the horses and men had to work. The horses hauling the wagons up to the front lines frequently became totally bogged down. It took Glubb's sappers twelve hours or more to clean up horses and wagons after some of the more desperate pushes. But throughout the diary there is constant concern for the welfare of the horses. Glubb's own horse Minx was a liver chestnut cob which he acquired when he first arrived in France. The very first day they were shelled three times before they got back to their billet. Glubb rode her everywhere: into Poperinghe for tea and to buy the papers, then straight back to the Front.

William Orpen's painting of a couple of mounted officers in the sunlit courtyard of the Hotel Sauvage in Cassel, in relaxed and carefree conversation with the locals, supports the image of normal life which Glubb conveys, even within sound of the shells and gunfire. Orpen was the best known and longest serving of the official war artists. A friend of the Commander in Chief, Douglas Haig, he received a knighthood for his work while the war was still on and had an enormously successful exhibition in London, entitled simply 'War', in 1918.

Orpen could create the brutal and gruesome images of the conflict which were the main feature of that show. But he also had an eccentric turn of mind and an eye for the comic and the ludicrous. He included two pictures of his French mistress Yvonne Aubicq, and after initially calling them *The Refugee* re-titled them *A Spy*. The military authorities were not amused, especially as Mata Hari had only recently, to the consternation of the British Press, been executed by the French. Orpen was recalled to London to explain himself.

Then, when the Armistice came, another caricature picture showed his attention caught by a soldier's glee club show, complete with pantomime horse and a marionette Kaiser. On the other hand, on Armistice night, Orpen would later recall he encountered a soldier maddened by the thought of going home to a jobless unknown future: 'The troops had gone through Hell, misery and terror of sudden death. Could one doubt that those at home would not reward them? Alas, Yes! The doubt has come true.'

As the Orpen painting suggests, all the business of ordinary life clung on in the towns behind the lines that had not been overrun. There were not only cafés and shops but cattle and horse markets and plenty of horse coping. John Glubb fell for a beautiful chestnut being offered by a Canadian. But when they tried it in the shafts of a wagon, the horse simply lay down. No deal.

The Courtyard, Hotel Sauvage, Cassel, Nord, William Orpen. (*Imperial War Museum, London, UK*)

Official Entry of the Kaiser, William Orpen. (*Pyms Gallery, UK*)

The horsemen took enormous pride in keeping up the appearance of their horses and wagons. Moving up to support an attack in early 1917, Glubb noted:

> I don't think I shall ever forget that sight, the steelwork of their harnesses gleaming like silver, their chains and traces swinging in and out, the sappers with clean shining badges, the horses with glossy coats and oil-softened leather work.

Glubb later describes how, during one of the pushes, the wagon drivers found themselves out of the mud and into more open country, where they spotted a field of clover:

> Scarcely had they dismounted than almost every driver was into the field picking great handfuls of clover for his horses. Old Driver Cannon, whose horses had been rather sick lately, kneeling down in his eagerness, pulled up great armfuls. Cannon is a London man. In peace time he used to drive one of those lovely pairs of horses you see pulling brewery vans.

Even close up to the front line, the practice was, when possible, to turn out the horses for a couple of hours in the morning with a few men to watch them. 'It was curious to see these bare hills covered with loose horses grazing, like herds of wild mustangs on the prairies.'

When his sections were pulled out of the line to prepare for the forthcoming attacks in the summer of 1917, Glubb's diary records scenes of bucolic bliss ('We used to ride out every morning on to the open grass hills. Here we allowed the horses to graze in a herd'). The drivers had spent the whole war riding the wagon horses at the walk, almost never even raising a trot. Now in this summer interval, Glubb started to teach them to jump and canter over some little brush fences:

> This alternated with periods of lying stretched in the long grass, the larks singing overhead. The horses wandered around, munching and swishing their tails, rolling with clumsy ponderance, or nipping one another for fun.

Glubb and the Engineers decided to organize a sports day on the local Souastre football field. After nearly three years of war, Glubb rejoices in 'quite a festive air':

> The day before the show was busy with preparing the field, marking the track with white tapes, erecting obstacles for the obstacle race, jumps for the officers' jumping, tents for guests. Slattery rode the bay mare Monchy, who can jump but is very wild. He could not hold her and she ran out several times. Minx took me round the four upright fences like a bird. As no one else had a clear round, this looked quite well. Unfortunately I had never tried her over water.

Feeds Round! Stable-time in the Wagon-lines, France, William Roberts. (*Imperial War Museum, London, UK*)

Three refusals, and Glubb and Minx were out! The most sensational event of the day was the Souastre Scurry, in which there were twenty-five entrants:

> The course was only four yards wide and included a hairpin bend … Altogether a most blood curdling event, the men all being bare backed on great lumbering draft horses. By a miracle no one was hurt.

Three weeks later, the sportsmen and their horses were summoned into the Third Battle of Ypres and Passchendaele.

In France, the Oxfords were alleged to be the first to play polo on their own horses. Inevitably, the Leicestershire Yeomanry were in the vanguard of the hunting fraternity. Four and a half couple of hounds inveigled out of the Quorn, the Cottesmore and Lord Harrington's, instilled a proper tone into proceedings, which had up to then involved a ragtag and bobtail assembly of French mutts persuaded to chase hares behind the lines.

But as the long months and then years of waiting for the dreamt-of 'Gap' to materialize, the echoes of equine Empire became ever more elaborate. The Indian cavalry regiments had shown their exquisite sense of splendour only two years before the War, when they were the prancing principals of the great Delhi Durbar for the new King and Emperor George V in 1912. Only a month before Passchendaele, eleven Indian cavalry regiments were again the star attraction at a horse show behind the lines, in which nearly fifty cavalry regiments took part, with displays, showing competitions, jumping and dressage which would have graced the Great Yorkshire Show. In Palestine there was even a hotly contested military Derby won by the Colonel of the Hussars, just returned from the third battle of Gaza – and handsomely rewarded with a splendid silver trophy obtained for the purpose from Cairo.

Even in the last few days before the crucial battles in France of March 1918, the Army was still up for a little sport. On the Sunday, the British 20th Division decided to put on an elaborate race meeting. General Gough himself showed up and entered two of his own horses – riding one of them in person and coming fourth out of a huge field of reportedly 120 animals. The General insouciantly compared his relaxation on the eve of the greatest battle of the entire war to Wellington's legendary ball on the night before Waterloo: 'I felt I had a good precedent for thus spending my Sunday afternoon.'

Just a week before, the 20th London division had staked out a racecourse on an airfield, with races from six furlongs to a mile, a Tote, bookies and wagon grandstands for the high-ups. One of their officers, Lieutenant E. M. Payne, described the sudden appearance of an apparently properly dressed London policeman – complete with truncheon – and a fully rigged out Pearly King, who then proceeded, to general hilarity, to tell General Gorringe that he was breaking the law by allowing unlicensed betting. There were races for draught horses, cavalry horses, and even one for mules, who were happy to join in the sport until they saw their stables and just leapt over the rails and headed for the feed buckets.

A Horse Ambulance Pulling a Sick Horse out of a Field, Edwin Noble. *(Imperial War Museum, London, UK)*

This exuberance was not allowed to impinge on the discipline of horse management. William Roberts' painting of the Wagon Lines is a picture of busy orderliness: brushing, picking out feet, sponging head and mouth. Roberts had served as a gunner in the Royal Artillery in the first part of the war. He had been an outstanding student at the Slade before the War and travelled widely in France and Italy where he had picked up the attachment to a Cubist style which is evident enough in this study. Roberts knew well enough the importance of discipline and the maintenance of appearance in the horse troops, which Glubb refers to. Roberts recorded the routine in a note about his painting:

> The order 'Feeds Round' is given by the sergeant major as a signal to cease grooming. The nose bags are then brought and placed just behind each horse where the men wait in readiness for the final order 'Feed'.

Given the huge numbers of animals pouring into France and Flanders with the Expeditionary Force, the Army and the vets had found it essential to impose this sort of discipline. Most of the troops in France had little or no experience of animal care. Almost straight away, the vets found themselves organizing 10-day courses for the troops on feeding, stable routine, correct fitting of saddlery and signs of disease or sickness. Through the war, and in circumstances of both retreat and advance, the evacuation, treatment and convalescence of horses became so well managed that losses of animals were extraordinarily low. During the War more than half a million horses were extracted from the battlefields. The process began with the animals being collected, often, as in Edwin Noble's painting, by a horse ambulance, and taken to an evacuation station. Thereafter they were taken, usually by rail, though sometimes by canal barge, to the veterinary hospitals, then on to convalescent depots. Entire trains were devoted in the wake of the Somme fighting in 1916 to evacuating equine casualties. At the height of the War, five hundred animals a day were being discharged as fit again and sent back to the Front. One day, early on, saw forty-eight trainloads of horses arrive back to be treated at the hospitals outside Calais. Another constant problem was giving horses in convalescence sufficient exercise. The vets resorted to using long ropes with horses tied on alternate sides and a man on horseback leading the tethered herd. The lack of exercise was a particular problem behind the trenches.

The German attack of March 1918 imposed ten days of incessant retreat. Everyone had to be ready to move at fifteen minutes' notice. The horses were never out of harness. They had to be groomed as best as could be managed. They were covering 25 miles a day, much of it at night. Yet, claims the Army Service Corps history, 'there was not a single case of gall or rub'.

When the final advance came in 1918, however, both the horses and the horsemen were insufficiently prepared. The vets found themselves dealing with hundreds of avoidable cases of harness galls and foot problems. They reported:

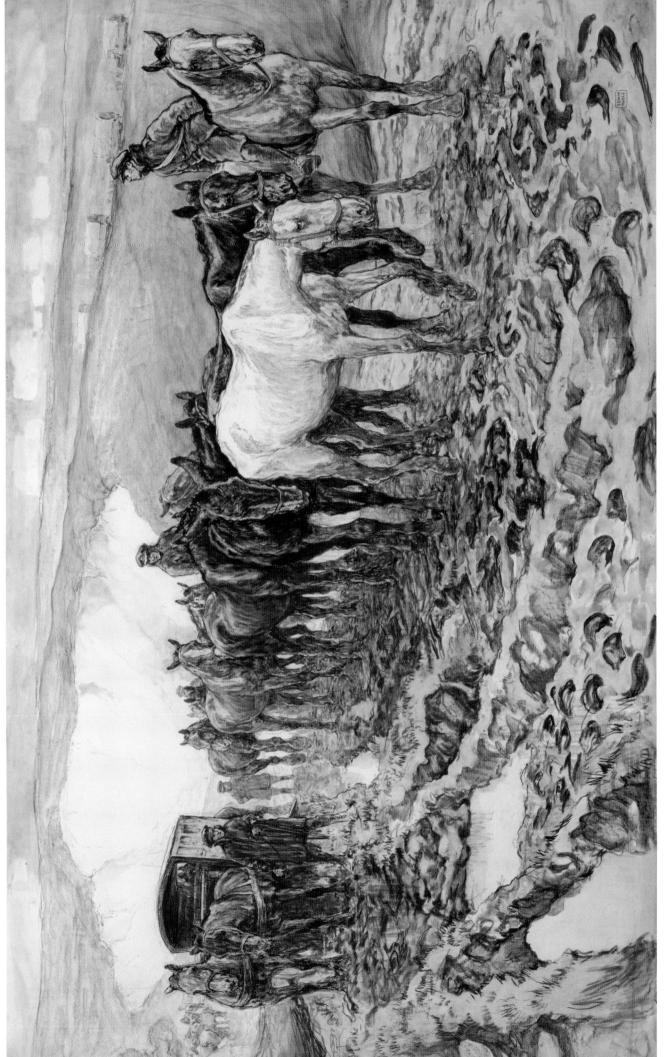

A Convoy of Sick Animals, Edwin Noble. *(Imperial War Museum, London, UK)*

These cases were attributable to marching heavy draught horses over hilly country in wet weather, harnessing up and moving off in the dark, insufficient application of dubbin, neglect of harness inspection and adjustments at halts on the line of march.

The vets knew that hard standing and cover were crucial to keeping animals in good condition and to their recovery after being invalided. They resorted to all sorts of initiatives, including buying a couple of great circus tents from owners who had found their entertainment business swallowed up by the fighting.

Edwin Noble's studies of sick horses were part of one of the most extensive contributions of all the war artists. Noble had himself been a sergeant in the Army Veterinary Corps. He travelled to America to record the activities of the British horse-purchasing teams, then came back to Europe to depict many of the afflictions the horses were enduring. He had studied at the Slade and was a teacher at Frank Calderon's school of animal painting. His rural scenes encompass paintings of sheep, ducks, cows, the whole range of domestic animals. In the middle of the war, in 1916, he was producing the most romantically bucolic scenes in posters for the London Underground.

Back on the Western Front the next year, he shows graphically some of the special problems his former colleagues in the Veterinary Corps had to confront, including the effects of poison gas. Horses enveloped in a gas attack were as vulnerable as humans. But there were also lingering effects. One vet in France recorded ninety-five cases – ten of which were to prove fatal – apparently caused by riders taking their horses over muddy ground which had been subjected to mustard gas attack. 'The animals,' he reported, 'get blistered about the feet, fetlocks, heels, thighs and sheaths, and occasionally about the eyes, several days after the shelling has taken place.' Some of the blisters were up to two feet square, and the animals became very lame. But treatment with whale oil and lead acetate was quite effective. Phosgene, the other lethal gas, affected mostly the lungs of horses. Some got over it, but many died a lingering death.

Recurrent afflictions which the horses suffered were lice and the various manifestations of mange, with all its skin irritations and lesions. These had to be treated in conventional ways through hygiene and rest, although there was the usual disagreement over the effect of clipping, which inevitably left the animals exposed to the trials of winter cold.

In the early days of the War in France, the horsemen and vets found themselves having to react to entirely new circumstances. Some of the problems seem comical. One vet complained there was simply too much galloping about:

Quite a number of individuals can be seen at all times galloping as if carrying important messages, yet from time to time they can pull up to talk to a friend or to watch the scene. Ammunition teams also in some instances travel long distances on hard ground at a fast gallop.

Mustard Gas, Edwin Noble. (*Imperial War Museum, London, UK*)

After a few trips they had to pull out exhausted animals. In the circumstances of the retreat from Mons, this vet felt they had gained nothing and 'done not a little to increase the general unsteadiness by their action'.

This concern for the effect of bad practice, not only on the horse and mule supply, but also on the morale of the troops, was a recurring theme of the vets. Large numbers of loose or wounded horses wandering around behind the lines contributed appreciably to the inevitable negative feelings during a retreat. One day in early September 1914, a vet team reported they had 'swept up over five hundred horses' and despatched them by rail to the temporary hospitals in the rear.

The vets were also rapidly coming to understand just how crucial were the right conditions for keeping horses in. The animals were mainly held in lines, with halters tied to a fixed rope. But poor halters often broke and allowed serious biting. Tethering the horses too closely allowed them to kick each other. Again, lack of hard standing produced widespread foot problems. Worse still, they were often highly visible to the enemy. Yet lines persisted as the most practical means of keeping horses throughout the war. Richard Carline's painting, on the Somme, was made only three months before the end of the war in August 1918, well in view of balloon observers from either side.

One vet team recorded more than a thousand casualties in one month, mostly from shell fire, but nearly a hundred and fifty from bombs. Indeed, a wagon and horses at Ypres were casualties of only the second ever bombing raid by a German plane. This vet team urged their people to use camouflage netting over old trenches and shell holes to shelter the horses. RAMC Private Cecil Warthin, driver of a horse-drawn ambulance at Ypres, kept his 'lovely little mare' in a corridor in a cellar beneath the ruined town, with just a nail in the wall to tie her to.

This sort of affection for the horses was extolled by the charities supporting the troops. The picture *Goodbye, Old Man* was commissioned by the Blue Cross from one of the most popular artists of the day, Fortunino Matania, and inspired not only donations but also poetry. Here is Henry Chappell:

Only a dying horse! Pull off the gear,
And slip the needless bit from frothing jaws,
Drag it aside there, leaving the roadway clear,
The battery thunders on with scarce a pause.
Prone by the shell-swept highway there it lies
With quivering limbs, as fast the life-tide fails,
Dark films are closing o'er the faithful eyes
That mutely plead for aid where none avails.
Onward the battery rolls, but one there speeds
Heedless of comrade's voice or bursting shell

Balloon Line on the Somme, Richard Carline. (*Imperial War Museum, London, UK*)

Back to the wounded friend who lonely bleeds
Beside the stony highway where he fell.
Only a dying horse! He swiftly kneels,
Lifts the limp head and hears the shivering sigh,
Kisses his friend, while down his cheek there steals
Sweet pity's tear, 'Goodbye, old man. Goodbye.'
No honours wait him, medal , badge, or star
Though scarce could war a kindlier deed unfold .
He bears within his breast, more precious far
Beyond the gift of kings, a heart of gold.

As well as the Blue Cross, the RSPCA very quickly lent its support to the Army and in the first few months delivered and erected four complete new hospitals in France. These were followed by another thirteen, with stabling for 12,500 horses.

As the War became more static, the vets began to build horse hospitals on an even more ambitious scale. One in the Pas-de-Calais was planned to take up to 30,000 stabled patients with turn-out paddocks and concrete standings. By the end of the War the Allies had built 70 horse hospitals capable, between them, of taking 100,000 horses and mules. The patients were usually shipped in from the Front by the trainload – up to five hundred at a time. They first had to go before a reception committee of vets, which assigned for destruction those they felt they could not cure. The survivors were sent on to the main hospital, where there was a rigorous regular programme of disinfection and sanitation. They were tethered to ropes, fed four times a day and medicated. But the authorities were not prepared to persist with treatment which did not produce quick results. Twice a week there was a Death Parade, in which each section of the hospital produced the animals they were recommending for destruction. A senior vet inspected them and, with few exceptions, authorized their fate.

The vets were often critical of the condition of the remounts that they received from England. One vet reported he had been sent to pick up 300 remounts. He was the only man in the troop who had a saddle; all the rest were to be halter-led by soldiers. But he rejected nearly half as footsore and left them behind to be rested and shod. There was a stampede in which a number of animals escaped, and he returned to the Front with only a fraction of the animals required.

These early experiences produced policies which were able to cope with the enormous demand. In one week in April 1917 there were 428,000 horses and mules in service, with 55,000 either in hospital or undergoing veterinary care, of which 2,600 were cured and despatched back to their units.

The hospitals contrived numerous imaginative ways to cope with the huge demands made of them. They developed the practice of exercising convalescent animals by tying up to twenty of them on either side of an extended rope. A mounted man led at the front and another kept

Opposite: *Goodbye Old Man*, watercolour, painted by Fortunino Matania (Italian, 1881–1963), showing a British soldier saying farewell to his dying horse. (*The painting was commissioned by The Blue Cross*)

the rope sufficiently taut at the back, in the Army's very original version of ride and lead. In many of the theatres of the War, vets found that simply turning the horses out was the quickest and most effective way of returning them to working condition.

From the beginning, there was always the problem of disposing of dead horses. Eventually, an entire department was set up, entitled the Disposals of Animals Branch. This organization was the channel through which horses were offloaded to French farmers, or sent for horse meat. They soon established their own butchery sections, each with a sergeant and three men. As the enormous toll of condemned or dead horses rose, the Branch set up what were known as 'carcase economisers'. They produced an official construction plan, with the 'slaughtering and cutting up floor' surrounded by stores for the products which were to be 'economised' – a hide store, a bone store, an oil tank, a feet tank, a meat tank and a fat melter. By the end of the war the Disposal of Animals Branch had earned the Army, even while the fighting was going on, more than £850,000. But in the first five months after the war's end, five times as much was realized in France alone.

Edwin Noble's picture of a rudimentary horse ambulance and its patient (see p.53) reflected a concern which during the retreat from Mons rapidly imposed itself on the front line vets. They simply had no means of transport. The system was, in theory, that equine casualties were dealt with by mobile vet units and then sent back to evacuating stations. From there they went back, usually by rail, to the veterinary hospitals. But as one front line vet put it, 'I am certain that, if a float were provided, a good many horses could be saved which with the present transport cannot be moved.' These pleas were eventually granted.

During the Mons retreat there were hundreds of animals left either running loose or unattended. One vet and his team had already found themselves with more than 600 spare cavalry horses when, as he put it:

I was requested to take charge of another 609 spare horses from the Indian Cavalry Brigade. Captain Hodgins and Lieutenant Pigeon were there to assist me, with one man to about six horses. Very short of picketing gear, not enough nosebags, and many loose horses with no means of securing them. We had to work very hard to be able to water once daily, feed three times, and exercise.

Chapter 5

The Desert

Germany inveigled the Turks into the War in November 1914. This was undoubtedly a triumph of diplomacy, long preparation and strategic sense. Though the apogee of Ottoman expansion had been reached at the gates of Vienna two and a half centuries earlier, the seeping away of Turkish imperial power had been slow and slight. The Turks still controlled almost all of what would now be called the Middle East, with the Russian Empire on their northern borders, and Britain, in Egypt, protecting the Suez Canal route to India to the south. The Germans had contrived to provide the Turks not only with modern arms but also with experienced army officers who advised, and even led, Turkish troops in the field.

Apart from Gallipoli, the war against the Turks separated quickly into two major campaigns: the first was to protect the Canal and then roll the enemy back up through Palestine; the second, known as the Mesopotamian campaign, was spurred on by the discovery of big new oilfields only a couple of years earlier. The latter started with a British attack on Basra in the Persian Gulf and an advance which was to culminate 500 miles inland in Baghdad, but only after the British had suffered their biggest military disaster since the American War of Independence, when 10,000 troops surrendered at the town of Kut and were led away, mostly to starvation and death.

These two campaigns were fought with horses on a scale quite beyond that of any other theatre. The cavalry were in constant action, patrolling, reconnoitring, charging into enemy positions, achieving astonishing feats of endurance in unconscionable heat or struggling through quagmires of winter mud and flood. These were theatres where some of the most skilled of the official war artists were able to record scenes of both camp and battle and depict the role of the horses.

At the time war broke out, the British seem to have been blithely insouciant about any threat to the most crucial of imperial sea routes, the Suez Canal. Although Ottoman troops were within a day's march of the Canal Zone, the one cavalry regiment and the horse artillery stationed in Egypt were immediately ordered to come home to England and prepare to join the British Expeditionary Force in France. They marched off to Port Said for embarkation, quite a few of the horses suffering from laminitis as a result of going through especially soft sand.

However, the prospect of Turkey joining the Germans produced rapid second thoughts, and India was required to despatch cavalry, camels and a thousand mules from the Mule Cart Corps. It was also realized that Egypt could be a useful staging post and base for training troops and animals coming from Australia and New Zealand to join the war effort.

The rush to join the colours had been as intense in Australia and New Zealand as anywhere in the Empire. The Australian government had to practically invent an army from scratch since they had previously had little other than militias, though Australians had fought in the Boer War. But in 1914 both infantry and mounted troops were required. Men came from all over the country to sign on, particularly stockmen from the cattle stations. One man was recorded as riding more than 400 miles to join up. The Australians were allowed, indeed encouraged, to enlist their horses as well as themselves. Technically, the horse was bought by the government and then given back to its rider.

Once these hardened stockmen got to Egypt and desert conditions, they showed endless initiative in looking after themselves and their horses. They always tried to carry extra water and a bag of spare feed. But they dumped everything else possible to reduce weight – even, as one man said, leaving his razor behind. When there were no stretchers available for their wounded, they devised a canvas sleigh, with a sword as the cross-stay, which was drawn behind the horse. On the march, whenever possible, there was a rigorous routine – forty minutes riding, ten minutes leading the horse and ten minutes rest. They were completely indifferent to uniform regulations. Men rode in breeches and singlets, even in shorts – although later in the war General Allenby stamped on this, because men were getting blood poisoning after their calves were rubbed raw.

By the time the Turks attacked the Suez Canal in February 1915 there were sufficient forces to turn them back – though not enough to undertake any effective pursuit. There followed nearly eighteen months in which there was mutual harassment along the hundred miles of the Canal's length but no major encounters.

In the meantime, however, the British in Egypt faced an unexpected alarm to the west, from Tripoli. This had been a possession of Britain's ally Italy, but the Italians had withdrawn all their forces there, and the Germans and Turks managed to beguile and bribe the local Bedouin and Senussi tribesmen to attack the British garrisons along the 700-mile western frontier of Egypt.

Defending this line involved some of the most trying conditions for horses that were to be encountered anywhere in the war. But it also proved to be very instructive to the British vets in coping with the tribulations to come in Palestine and Mesopotamia. Above all there was the search for water. There were more than 1,000 horses and 150 mules to be watered, yet even when wells were found, the water could be so brackish that the horses would only drink a little and rapidly lost condition. The soft sand so exhausted the animals that after one day's march they had to be rested the next day. There was no question of pursuing a fleeing enemy. Then, when the rains came, the desert turned into a sea of mud. In these quagmires movement was virtually impossible.

The cavalry horses became exhausted. In the four months of the campaign nearly half had to be withdrawn for treatment, or hospitalized. Fortunately, a great number of them could be brought back to the veterinary hospitals at Alexandria. They had suffered sand colic and digestion problems, along with respiratory illnesses and severe loss of condition.

The Wells at Samaria, James McBey. (*Imperial War Museum, London, UK*)

Extraordinarily, only two per cent died. The rest were able to recover and rejoin a campaign which ended at Easter 1916 with the subjugation of the Senussi and the capture of their leaders.

When the push up through the Sinai desert and into Palestine began in 1916 the horses were central to the military strategy, and their management became crucial. The effect of poor water was even more severe. Horses simply would not drink sufficient water if the supply was at all sour or brackish, though mules were more resilient. Whole brigades of cavalry had to be brought back to fresh-water areas, where they took up to three weeks to recover. Wells had to be constantly tested for salinity, because horses would drink saline water but then become ill. Eventually, as the British armies advanced, a pipeline with pumping stations followed them, and indeed largely governed the pace at which the army's progress could take place.

Through the desert there is practically no vegetation, just dunes and hills of shifting sand. All the horses' feed had to accompany them on the backs of mules and camels, along with the ammunition and other supplies. Fit horses proved remarkably resilient to the desert heat, which reached up to 117° Fahrenheit, and to the dense dust storms of May and June. But the minute they started to sicken or lose condition their decline would be rapid.

When the cavalry and horse artillery had left for France in September 1914, Egypt had been effectively denuded of military horses. The turnaround in the following twelve months was extraordinary. By December of 1915 there were 44,000 horses and mules under the Army's muster in the country.

Through 1915, the war in the Middle East was dominated by the brutal encounters in Gallipoli. But the British did try two forward thrusts from the Canal Zone, aiming to deter any renewed attack on the Canal. Both failed at considerable cost. The Worcester Yeomanry lost 100 men and more than 400 horses in one engagement, and the Warwicks and Gloucester Yeomanry lost three entire squadrons either killed or taken prisoner.

These setbacks and the experience in the Western Desert demonstrated that any operations up through Turkish-occupied Palestine would be utterly reliant on horses and would have to be meticulously planned to ensure there was sufficient water and supplies to sustain an advance.

James McBey, illegitimate son of a blacksmith's daughter from Aberdeen, was already a renowned portrait painter when he was sent out to Egypt in June 1917. Within two months he had produced sixty-eight water colours 'mounted and ready for despatch to the War Office'. By the War's end he had amassed more than three hundred paintings, including the most celebrated drawing of Lawrence of Arabia. But the horses of the desert war were his principal preoccupation.

The enduring legend which Lawrence created, through *Seven Pillars of Wisdom*, of the Arabs as Britain's gallant friends and allies in the War, is hugely misleading. In fact, throughout the four years of the Turkish campaigns, Arab horsemen, deft and finely mounted, were a constant source of trouble for the British and Indian cavalry, harassing retreats and constantly prepared to fade away if attacked themselves, then returning to the fray.

Cavalry in Coastal Sector, James McBey. (*Imperial War Museum, London, UK*)

After the disastrous surrender of Kut, the British set about building up an overwhelming advantage of numbers in Mesopotamia which eventually was to succeed not only in ousting the Turks from Kut but also taking Baghdad and rolling the enemy back to Anatolia itself.

The Mesopotamian campaign – in modern Iraq – was controlled from India, with responsibility handed to the Indian Army and Indian Civil Service. Indeed, they had arrangements in train for a force of occupation even before Turkey entered the war.

The troops who went to Mesopotamia constituted a roll call of legendary Indian regiments, their reputations forged in the wars in Afghanistan and the North West Frontier: Hodson's Horse, the Begum of Bhopal's regiment, the 3rd Punjab Cavalry, Watson's Horse, the Hariana Lancers, the Rohilkand Horse, the Bengal Cavalry.

They found themselves, initially, in almost perfect horse country in the plains of the Fertile Crescent between the Tigris and Euphrates rivers. Captain Eve of the 13th Hussars wrote: 'Horses do wonderfully well here and look and are as fit as fleas.' Relatively undisturbed, the troops were soon organizing polo matches and packs of hounds to hunt jackals. There was even an extraordinary moment when a hundred Cossacks appeared out of the northern hills, having ridden more than 200 miles across Ottoman territory to join their British allies. This unique feat proved short lived, for after a fortnight of dining and entertainment, and the presentation of Military Crosses to the Cossack officers, they set off and successfully made it back to their own lines. This may well have been the only direct contact between the forces of the British and Russian Empires before the 1917 revolution took the Russians out of the War.

For the cavalry moving forward to the desert and the next stages of the Mesopotamian campaign, the idyll of the Fertile Crescent rapidly evaporated. Failure to burn refuse, as well as horse droppings and the unburied carcases of dead animals, produced plagues of sand flies, lice and mosquitoes, descending in clouds on men and horses. Troops and animals could only be protected with total coverage of netting and masks. Movement of the animals was challenging, but with the cooperation of the Royal Navy, the authorities came up with an enterprising solution. Two barges were roped to the side of each of four river steamers and the horses were slung on to them, secured along a rope with their heads facing outwards at the water. With 90 horses in each barge, plus forage, the flotilla could take more than 700 animals at a time. The theoretical efficiency of this scheme soon evaporated, however. Horses broke free, several went over the side and drowned and there was much kicking and biting, to say nothing of the hazards to men trying to feed and water them.

As the advance towards Kut began, the cavalry were called on to undertake reconnaissance and harass the Arab horsemen. Two days before Christmas, the 7th Cavalry covered 70 miles in two days on one of these sorties, without managing to water the horses at all. When action finally came at a Turkish defensive position at a place called Lajj, the British and Indian cavalry found themselves facing field guns, trenches and machine guns. Nevertheless, a classic cavalry charge ensued. Guy Pedder, a young officer in the first wave, was wounded in the arm and lost his horse just a few yards from the main Turkish trenches. As he stood there he saw the

Hodson's Horse at Aleppo, James McBey. (Imperial War Museum, London, UK)

next squadron come galloping in. 'It was a sight I shall never forget,' he said later. 'The leader to the fore with sword aloft, the line of panting horses, the grim eager faces of the men, the flashing swords.' The leader was Captain Eve, mounted on his mare Caprice. Pedder held up his shattered arm. Echoing the famous exchange between Wellington and the Earl of Uxbridge at Waterloo, Eve shouted, 'Hard lines, old boy. Never mind.'

Moments later, plunging across the Turkish trenches, Eve was unhorsed and killed. Caprice ran loose and disappeared. Pedder made it back to the British lines.

Caprice was to become one of the most celebrated horses of the War. More than a year later, Captain Eve's groom, Private Hogg, meeting some Indian troops in Baghdad, heard a most insistent whinny. It was Caprice. Evidently, from her scars, she had suffered seven bullet wounds and been in Turkish hands or wandering the desert for an unknown length of time before the Indians picked her up. She was restored to the regiment, and after the War went to live out the rest of her days with Captain Eve's widow in Surrey.

For the cavalry coming by ship from India the Mesopotamia campaign had had an inauspicious opening. A squadron of Queen Victoria's Own Light Cavalry were first off the boat. As soon as they got to camp the horses stampeded – more than a hundred of them – and very few were recovered. Early plunder for the locals, no doubt.

Within a month or so the remainder of the regiment had their first experience of what this campaign was going to entail. They were required to charge against some advancing Turkish positions. 'Charge', in fact, actually meant wading through a series of *wadis* and streams three or four feet deep, and then getting stuck in a marsh. Major Anderson found himself 'in a very unpleasant situation standing waist deep in water under heavy fire'. He had two horses shot from under him. However, he then had the satisfaction of pursuing an escaping Turk and noting 'it is wonderful how easily a sword goes in'.

The first major action, in early March, introduced the troops to some of the hazards which awaited them. Even eight-horse teams could not move guns through the sand; a sandstorm arose; and then came the first of the mirages which were to deceive regularly throughout the campaign, with troops unable to discern whether the enemy were mounted, or even existed at all.

The Arab horsemen then made their first appearance, dashing in on the flanks and off again. 'The Arabs,' wrote one British officer, 'could always outpace our cavalry.' When the Turks tried to retake Basra, there were as many as 10,000 of these Arab irregulars in their force. At one point, the 7th Lancers were ordered to attack some entrenched positions in a date palm grove. It was an old-fashioned charge across 1,000 yards of open but heavy ground. 'We got in to them with the lance,' recorded Captain Boys-Stones. 'We did tremendous execution. I remember losing my sword in an Arab and dismounting to pull it out of him.'

Throughout the war, the British and Indian cavalry found great difficulty in dealing with the Arabs. One officer, lamenting that the Arab horsemen could outpace his best polo pony, noted that they needed to be very close up to do any damage in a charge, as their practice was to fire while mounted. But their numbers made them very dangerous, and they were able to break off an engagement and escape whenever they chose. Captain George Boys-Stones, who was Adjutant of the Indian 7th Lancers, again described 'tremendous swarms of Arab cavalry' coming at them during a retreat. The pack horses had bolted, along with two of the officer's chargers. The whole day was spent trying to fend off what Boys-Stones estimated as more than 5,000 Arab horsemen, before the artillery managed to get things under control.

The Turks having tried to reach the Suez Canal in the first months of 1915 and been repulsed, it still took the next three years to force them back over the Sinai desert, past Gaza, and eventually to Jerusalem and on to Damascus. Throughout this immense campaign, the British and Imperial armies were almost totally dependent on horses and camels. There were few metalled roads where motor vehicles could operate, and the few tanks which appeared in 1917 could not cope with conditions and were all knocked out.

Throughout these three years there were, at any one time, 60,000 horses in the field, nearly half of them cavalry, an equal number of mules and donkeys and as many camels. The challenges they faced were unprecedented. It could take fourteen horses to haul a gun through the soft sand. Horses went up to three days without water while involved in continuous reconnaissance and action. They had to go for days on end with as little as four pounds of grain per day – and no hay.

As always, water was the greatest problem. The whole of the four-year war had to be planned around the availability of water. The enemy, as they were forced back, destroyed wells whenever they could. The Royal Engineers followed the advancing troops, building a water pipeline and pumping stations, as well as a railway, eventually all the way from Egypt to Jerusalem. When the British were planning their final assault on Gaza, the calculation was that 400,000 gallons a day were needed – 500 tons weight – just to support the right wing of the attack. The heat was so great that their rifles blistered the men's hands. It could be up to and beyond 115° Fahrenheit.

Yet the horses proved remarkably resilient. During the Romani battle, some horses were not watered for almost three days. They also withstood shelling with remarkable fortitude. Exceptional veterinary care and horsemastership kept disease at bay in the desert. Animals that lost condition were funnelled back through field veterinary stations to recuperate in Egypt. In the last months of the war, the cavalry had nearly 30,000 horses in the field and advanced over 400 miles in a series of major charges and battles, yet lost fewer than 4,000 animals.

Care evolved rapidly in the adverse conditions. To give protection from flies, manes and tails were not clipped, but coats were, whenever possible, as part of the fight against mange. Sick horses were evacuated, at the first sign of symptoms, to the base vet hospitals, as were horses that lost condition. Sand colic was an ever present hazard. When horses got on to green fields in the Jordan valley, they expelled huge amounts of sand in their droppings. Yet, at the end of long marches they still had enough strength left for cavalry charges of up to two miles over sand and scrub.

Trooper Cady Hoyte of the Warwickshire Yeomanry, in a recently discovered diary, gives a vivid insight into life with the horses in the Sinai desert campaign. The lines where the horses were tethered in regulation fashion were intermittently targeted by Turkish planes:

Almost every morning at precisely the same time, Turkish planes would come over and pay us a visit. At the first sign of their approach we had to run and untie our horse, mount and ride out of camp as quickly as possible. The idea was to get the horses as scattered as possible before the bombs fell.

Hoyte and the Warwickshires soon found themselves patrolling and engaged in action against the Turks. In these encounters the Yeomanry were usually dismounted, with their horses concealed in gullies and behind rocks in the desert. After one fierce action in which the Turks prevailed, Hoyte found himself pelting back to the horses and galloping off amid gunfire, surrounded by many of his captured or killed comrades' riderless horses. 'For hours we rode back, but now both horses and men were nearly frantic with thirst.' They came at last to some palms and a well. 'In spite of all orders, the horses became almost uncontrollable, and many of the men too.'

Sometimes the action would be mounted. Hoyte describes the arc of horsemen which would precede the main troop, always the first enemy target. One night, they and their horses had to pick their way in the dark through a grove of trees reportedly occupied by Turks:

What a pleasant thing to do! In pitch darkness, with just a sword for protection, to ride for something like half a mile through a thick palm grove in the middle of the desert, with the chance of finding a Turk lurking behind every tree!

Water, again, was the constant concern. One night when the order came to get mounted and move out, Hoyte could not find his mare. He was stranded.

Then I remembered that just before we halted we had crossed a shallow *wadi* in which there were small pools of water. Walking back through the darkness and calling out her name, I eventually saw the dim outline of a horse coming towards me, and sure enough it was my mare. I felt her muzzle, and it was quite wet. She had found a drink.

Another time Hoyte became hopelessly lost around El Arish. Eventually, he just dropped the reins and consigned his fate to the mare, who took him safely back to the camp. 'Never before had I realized,' he wrote, 'what a pal a horse could be.'

Hoyte ended his time in Palestine taking part in the charge against the Turks in the capture of Beersheba. The Warwickshires overran the Turkish positions, sabreing the gunners but losing a quarter of their own men and horses. It was then back through the desert to Egypt and a forced and emotional farewell to their horses.

The Charge of the Australian Light Horse at Beersheba, George Lambert (Australian War Memorial, Canberra, Australia)

While the cavalry fretted behind the lines in Flanders, or fought dismounted in the trenches, death and glory were available in abundance to the mounted troops in Palestine and Mesopotamia. The painting by George Lambert immortalises the most dashing act of determined bravery in the whole of the desert war – the charge at Beersheba.

With its railway line and water wells, Beersheba stood in the way of General Allenby's advance through Palestine towards Jerusalem and then Damascus. Even to get within sight of Beersheba, the horsemen had to make their way through unmapped and arid desert for two days. On the last night of their ride, 30 October, the mounted division kept going through the featureless landscape all night, to emerge at daylight within five miles of Beersheba. Many of the horses had not been watered for thirty-six or even forty-eight hours. In Beersheba it was known that there were at least seventeen wells, and it was evident that the town had to be taken, or else there would be a parching, probably lethal, retreat.

Beersheba was guarded by two hills and Turkish positions which proved hard to subdue. By four o'clock, with only an hour of daylight left, the Australian General Chauvel, in conference with his two Light Horse brigade commanders, decided that only a frontal assault could carry the day.

The horsemen were faced with a range of Turkish trenches four to six feet wide, clusters of the fearful cavalry pits (conical holes with spikes at the bottom into which a galloping horse could plummet) and machine guns and artillery.

In a matter of minutes, the horsemen, armed with rifle, pistol and bayonet, were drawn up in line abreast about a mile and a half from the Turkish trenches. They set off at a trot, then sped up to a canter and for the last mile or more a full gallop. Trooper Scotty Bolton remembered reaching down and unsheathing his bayonet at full gallop. His horse Monty took a bullet that scarred his quarters. But they carried on and leaped clean over the first Turkish trenches. A watching officer remembered:

A most inspiring sight. It was growing dark and the enemy trenches were outlined in fire by the flashes of their rifles. In front the long lines of cavalry swept forward at racing speed, half obscured in clouds of reddish dust. Amid the deafening noise all around, they seemed to move silently like some splendid swift machine.

Another trooper, Ion Idriess, recalled:

The last half mile was a berserk gallop with the squadrons in magnificent line, the horses leaping the redoubt trenches, with the Turkish bayonets thrusting up for the bellies of the horses.

Two squadrons of the 12th Light Horse jumped all the trenches and hurtled on for half a mile into the town of Beersheba itself. Most of the troops, as they were trained, leaped from their horses and engaged the Turkish defenders with pistol and bayonet. The Turks, terrified of the

Battle of Romani, 4 August 1916, George Lambert. (*Australian War Memorial, Canberra, Australia*)

Australian cavalry, as their commander Ismet Bey was later to put it, largely broke, with many killed and large numbers surrendering.

Trooper Bolton, in civilian life a Geelong engine driver, found himself in a street where he saw, in the window of a house, a German officer working a switchboard. Bolton leaped from his horse and took the German at pistol point. It turned out he had been controlling the detonators which had been placed in the town's wells. All but two of the wells were to be found intact. Back on his horse, Bolton saw another German officer and half a dozen men galloping away with a field gun. Bolton caught them, felled the officer with his pistol, and the gun crew surrendered with their weapon.

The horsemen took large numbers of prisoners. Staff Sergeant A. J. Cox of the Australian 4th Horse, was found, all on his own, with forty prisoners and their machine gun. As darkness came, the rest of the Desert Mounted Corps swept into town, with the Turkish troops fleeing desperately.

Beersheba fell, the horses and men were watered and the road was opened up for the eventual advance towards Jerusalem. Of the 500 Light Horsemen who took part in the charge 31 were killed and 36 wounded. More than 400 of the horses, most of them Walers, the sturdy products of the Australian outback, also survived.

The war in Palestine produced extraordinary feats of derring-do and bravery, but fearsome carnage amongst the horses. The mounted squadrons – from the English county regiments as well as the Australians and New Zealanders – were equipped with rifles as well as sabres, and accompanied by machine gun units. They faced Turks equipped with the latest German artillery and machine guns as well as rifles. Yet repeatedly throughout the Palestinian campaign, the horsemen attacked and overcame the most modern firepower available.

But the cost could be daunting. At the battle of Huj, near Gaza, in November 1917, the Allies came up against a sizeable Turkish force of infantry dug in, with machine guns and field artillery operated by Austrian and German gunners. The British commander decided that an attack by the Worcestershire and Warwickshire Light Horse was the appropriate response. And so it was that some 170 men set off at full gallop across the best part of a mile of desert and finally up a severe slope to wreak their havoc. Their only weapons were their drawn sabres. The enemy's 75mm guns and machine guns continued firing until the range was point blank, but the horsemen rode right through the guns, sabreing their crews and running down the fleeing infantry.

Then suddenly, as one of the British medical officers, Captain Teichman, recorded, 'The terrific din of shrieking and exploding shells ceased.' The engagement was over. The Germans and the Austrians lay dead and wounded beside their guns. The British dead and wounded lay scattered around and beyond the gun batteries. 'Our squadrons had not fired a shot and every single casualty we inflicted was caused by our sword thrusts,' Captain Teichman noted, before recording with professional wonderment, 'One could not help contrasting the clean wounds caused by our sword thrusts with the ghastly wounds sustained by our men from shell fire and saw-bayonet.'

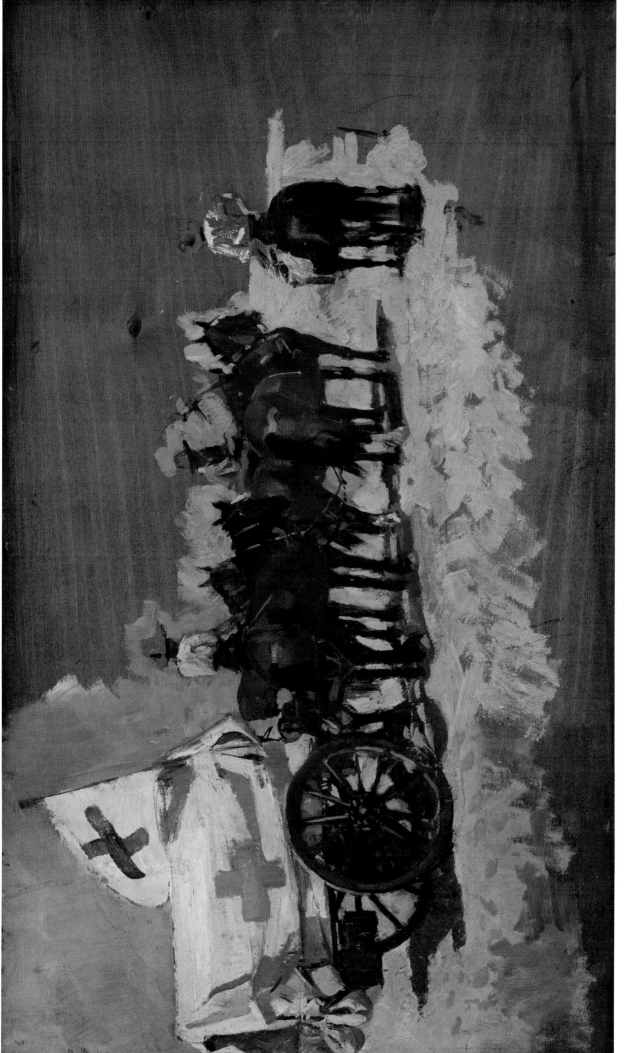

Sand Cart and Team, Kantara, George Lambert. (Australian War Memorial, Canberra, Australia)

The Warwicks and the Worcesters had lost a quarter of their men. But the human losses told just part of the tale of battle, for only about 30 of the 170 horses survived. In the world of the 75mm gun and the modern machine gun, it was the greater bulk of the horse which offered the biggest target and the easiest sacrifice. Yet, in this new era of industrialized warfare, the awesome sight of charging cavalry could still overwhelm even a steadfast foe.

In the final push towards Damascus, there were further extraordinary feats: the 4th Cavalry covered 70 miles in 34 hours, fought two actions and lost only 26 horses; the 3rd Australian Light Horse at one point covered 11 miles in 70 minutes; a British cavalry brigade covered 50 miles in 22 hours; in eleven breathtaking days at the end of September, the Allied cavalry advanced 200 miles, capturing 60,000 prisoners, 140 guns and 500 machine guns.

Lambert's picture of the Battle of Romani marks one of the most desperate and most crucial episodes of the desert war. The German General Kress, in charge of the Turkish troops, had, by marching only at night for twenty-five days, crept up on the Australian and New Zealand troops guarding the Suez Canal. It was only when an Australian officer hitched an aeroplane ride that the advance was discovered. In the intense heat of the summer, Kress had not only brought up his troops but also transported his guns on an ingenious rubber-tyred device called a 'pedrail', which delivered much better progress through the sand.

The battle began in the night of 3 August, with the Turkish infantrymen shouting, 'Finish Australia!' as they rushed forward. The fighting stretched over a front of ten miles or more, with the Australian and New Zealand mounted troops being deployed in constant movement. Colonel John Royston, a South African who commanded the Australian 2nd Brigade, was said to have used up fourteen horses during the battle before he was finally wounded and had to give up. It was not until 9 August that Kress and the Turks finally retreated.

Lambert, an Englishman born in St Petersburg and whose family had emigrated to Australia, was extraordinarily prolific after being appointed an official Australian war artist in 1917. He had a most sympathetic eye for the work of the horses and of their riders. *With the Remounts* is as exuberant a picture as any from the desert artists. *The Sand Cart Team*, is in its different way as emotive a representation of the trials of the hot plains. Lieutenant Colonel Michael Bruxner, who had the job of hosting Lambert in Egypt, described him as 'a magnificent horseman himself, who could hold his own with our finest riders. No one ever objected to lending his charger to our guest.' In return, Lambert painted Bruxner's charger Rainbow, a handsome chestnut carrying his officer's saddle and wallet and a fine example of the Australian horses which survived the rigours of the desert so well.

The campaign in Palestine and Egypt had seen the Turks initially sweep down almost to the banks of the Suez Canal — and get within an ace of severing the Imperial route to India — but then be driven back through the deserts of Gaza, Palestine and Syria as far north as Aleppo. This confrontation with the Ottoman Empire demanded epic endurance, constant improvisation and initiative and a vast supply of animals — camels, as well as horses and mules and, in the last phase of the war, the more than 12,000 Egyptian donkeys who trekked all the way to the cold and the mountains of Judaea.

Rainbow, Troop Horse, George Lambert. (*Australian War Memorial, Canberra, Australia*)

There were more than 100,000 horses and mules engaged in the Palestine war at any one time. Attrition was severe: more than 9,000 horses and nearly 2,000 mules were killed even in the successful last six months of campaigning. Food, forage and water were a constant problem – especially water. Going without water for two days was common. The gallant Bucks and Dorsets went three days and the Lincoln Yeomanry once reported going 84 hours without watering their animals while on the march. The whole Palestine campaign depended on being able to locate and secure a supply of water. After Huj, an attempt was made to ration the amount of water by imposing a time limit on each batch of horses as they came to the troughs. But the plan was a disaster as the animals, who had been without a drink for nearly two days, got out of control and rushed the troughs. As the troops continued their advance, water again ran short and horses had to be sent back up to 30 miles for watering.

The Allied armies had learned hard lessons from the start of the war, as the early encounters with the Turks in the desert country of Sinai often turned on the defence or destruction of wells. The progress of the war in Palestine was fitful, dogged by the demands of other theatres – the huge effort in Gallipoli, the fighting in Salonika in northern Greece and the demand for troops to be diverted to the Western Front. After the debacle at Gallipoli, the main port of Alexandria saw ships arriving every day for six weeks with the equine casualties and refugees.

As the army advanced through Sinai, the supply lines of horses, mules and camels carrying water became very extended. The heavy Sinai sand was particularly hard on the horses dragging the artillery. Many lost condition quickly and died. It was here that the vets opening them up for post mortem found enlarged hearts. One vet wrote sadly:

> It appears to have been overlooked that the artillery horse had to carry nearly the same weight as the cavalry, and had at the same time to assist in dragging a gun weighing a ton and a half. Yet there were many instances where a brigade, in their eagerness to attack, advanced at such a rapid pace that the horse artillery were unable to keep up with them and support them.

Beside the lack of water, there were constant problems with feed supply and forage. For months, even years, the horses never saw grass or any greenery. It was only when the troops finally broke out of the Sinai that the horses found a promised land. At first the advance was through such heavy sand that double teams were required for the gun and ammunition wagons. It was past dark when the halt was called on the first day, and the men lay down to try and snatch a few hours sleep with the reins of the horses through their arms. This was established practice in the desert, where there was no grazing and the horses were content to stand quietly while their riders slept. But this first night out of El Arish, the horses soon began to pull and snatch at the reins and try to wander away, and the soldiers woke to realize they had arrived among the first green planted crops they had encountered in months. Sleep was abandoned in favour of indulging their horses to the full.

Charge of the 2nd Lancers at El Afuli: in the Valley of Armageddon, 5am, Friday 20 September 1918, Thomas Dugdale. (*Imperial War Museum, London, UK*)

The Allied armies were stalled for many months after a failed attack on Gaza. But when the advance was resumed in the winter through the Jordan valley and up to the hills of Judaea, the horses suffered greatly from cold. They were advancing up steep hillsides on little more than goat tracks and enduring constant enemy rifle fire. The veterinary services were under intense pressure. More than 82,000 horses and mules were registered as requiring their attention in the first six months of 1918. The situation had been just as bad in the previous year, and was to stay the same till the end of the war.

General Allenby's advance in 1918 took the army up along the coast to Haifa and then turned inland on the road to Damascus. Thomas Dugdale's painting of the 2nd Lancers records the action to take a key village along the railway line at El Afule. One of the 2nd Lancers, Captain D. E. Whitworth, left a personal description of this flamboyant charge. He was making his way, following the route on his map towards the river Kishon, when he saw two columns of Turks about 200 yards away.

The men saw the enemy at the same moment. They all saw red and broke into a hell for leather gallop. Before I realized it, we were right on top of the enemy. I saw a young Turk aiming at me. I realized I was still holding my map and had forgotten to draw my sword. The little brute missed me and tried to jab his rifle in my stomach. I had just time to draw and thrust. The point got him in the neck and he went down like a house of cards. I made for another Turk. My point caught him plumb between the shoulders and the shock nearly dislocated my arm – perhaps he was wearing a pair of steel braces. During all this I saw little of what was going on around me. I only remember my orderly Lal Chand, on my second horse Advocate, who had the regimental flag furled round his lance, dragging a Turk along the ground who had got stuck on the point.

As the action ended, Whitworth discovered that not a single man in his squadron had even been wounded. Nor had they lost any horses. Within the hour the 2nd Lancers had galloped into El Afule town and captured not only the railway station but three German aeroplanes – and then a fourth, who landed having apparently failed to notice that the airfield had changed hands.

As the Turkish armies disintegrated, the vets were faced with new problems. One eyewitness wrote:

When the enemy receives such a terrific bombardment, followed up by devastating machine gun fire and bombing by low flying aeroplanes, as happened in these operations, the situation becomes a pandemonium during which animals are abandoned and allowed to stampede in every direction. In the narrow gorge which leads from Tul Keram to Nablus, the scene of destruction among the enemy was frightful and will never be forgotten by those who witnessed it. Those who escaped death and wounds soon abandoned guns, animals and everything and took to the hills. When those animals who

The Machine Gun Section: Cheshire Yeomanry, Going into Action in Syria, W.P. Moss. (*Imperial War Museum, London, UK*)

escaped with their lives were captured, many were wounded and nearly all of them were in such a wretched emaciated condition as to be worthless for military purposes.

Through the month of October 1918, 4,900 captured animals were brought down to the receiving stations, many ridden or led by prisoners of war. Hundreds were too weak or exhausted to travel and were shot.

The dreadful symmetry of mechanized destruction and improbably dashing bravery continued right through the war in Palestine and Syria. As the armies approached Damascus in 1918, a unit of New Zealand machine gunners and a detachment of French troops reached an escarpment at the top of the Barada Gorge. The gorge is a sinuous valley with almost vertical cliff walls. Along the valley floor runs both the main road and the railway from Damascus to Beirut. As the New Zealanders and the French looked down, they saw thousands of men and horses with wagons and guns winding their way along the narrow defile. One of the New Zealanders described what happened next as 'one of the most frightful tragedies of the campaign'. Sergeant Kirkpatrick recalled:

We quickly took up positions almost invisible to the dense mass of enemy below. The head of the column was felled and, as the unfortunates behind kept pressing forward, they were mown down by some invisible scythe. Horses and men went down together in hundreds and died in one tangled bleeding mass.

Thousands turned back up the valley towards the city, only to run into Australian troops, who finished the job. The dead were unnumbered, but the Australians took 4,000 prisoners. It took days to burn and blast a way through the corpses, the animal carcasses and the wrecked wagons to reopen the road to Damascus.

Meanwhile, a troop of British cavalry swept past and right into the centre of Damascus, led by the legendarily dashing Lieutenant Charles Foulkes Taylor (six months earlier he had galloped his men right through the Turkish lines at Es Salt, captured a German officer and subdued another by hitting him over the head with a pistol. His troopers had taken 200 prisoners – all with just bayonet and sword.) Now joined by Lieutenant A.N.C. Olden of the Australian Light Horse, and his adjutant, he forced his way through milling crowds to the Serai, Damascus's Town Hall, and reined their chargers to a halt. There then followed the most extraordinary scene.

'Where is the Governor?' the officers demanded.

'He awaits you in the Hall above,' came the response from an English-speaking official.

The officers dismounted, handed their horses to three troopers and, pistols in hand, bounded up the stairs, to be greeted by Emir Said el Kabir, the City Governor, with the words: 'In the name of the City of Damascus, I welcome the first of the British Army.'

'Does the city surrender?' demanded Olden.

Entering Damascus: Australians Galloping along the Beyrout Road, James McBey. (*Imperial War Museum, London, UK*)

'Yes. There will be no further opposition in the city,' replied the Emir.

And so the intrepid trio took the submission of the largest city in the region, instructing the Governor to issue orders to the police to prevent looting and to inform the 10,000 or more Turkish troops in the city that they would have to lay down their arms.

The painting of the Charge at El Mughar, commissioned in tribute to some who took part, hangs on the wall of the Institute of Directors in London. It is by James Beadle, the son of an Indian Army officer, who was already a renowned battle painter before the War broke out. He portrays here the most brilliantly executed cavalry charge of the Palestine War, in November 1917.

Cavalry manuals decreed that 600 yards was about the maximum distance that horsemen should be asked to charge. At El Mughar, the Bucks, the Berks and the Dorsets covered the best part of two miles and overwhelmed the opposing Turkish machine gunners and infantry. They captured more than 1,000 officers and men, as well as field guns and machine guns. About 2,000 Turks were killed or wounded, while the British lost only 16 men, though the toll of horses (more than 200) was greater.

Yet the attack had looked a most perilous project when the situation was reconnoitred earlier in the day. Lieutenant Cyrus Perkins of the Bucks had been despatched forward across the desert, only to find himself followed by machine gun bullets 'like a spotlight follows a dancer', as a comrade wrote. He cantered all the way across the Turkish front unscathed, but could find none of the dips or gullies which the cavalry usually required to give cover in getting close to the enemy. When he reported all this to General Godwin, the commander simply said: 'Then we'll gallop it.'

And so they did – three waves of horsemen hurtling across the rocks and sand. Lieutenant Perkins wrote afterwards:

As the enemy's fire hotted up, it became harder to hold the horses to the trot, so gradually the pace quickened. As we neared the ridge, swords were drawn and very soon we were breasting the rise with their gun blasts feeling like pillows hitting one's face. Then in seconds they were all around us, some shooting, some scrambling out of slip trenches and some sensibly falling flat on their faces. It had taken us, I suppose, a bit over five minutes. Blown and galloping horses are hard to handle one-handed while you have a sword in the other. One missed and missed again until the odd Turk wasn't quite quick enough. In just such a case, the hours spent in arms drill paid off, for one instinctively leaned well forward and remained so to offset the jerk as the sword comes out, in fact precisely as one had so often been told.

When I went to collect my men beyond the ridge, I found Corporal Blades quite composed, as a good ex-Bobby should be, penning 200 or more Turks in a quarry, while literally hundreds more were fleeing down to the plain below.

Charge at El Mughar, J.P. Beadle. (Defence Academy of the UK/ Roy Fox)

The whole action took only about fifteen minutes.

The desert war produced various bizarre methods of combat. On one occasion a troop of British Yeomanry, pursuing some fleeing Turkish horsemen, apparently grabbed them by the collar and pulled them off their horses, before taking them prisoner. More ruthlessly, some were sabred right through at the gallop.

But there were long quiescent periods when the race meetings and gymkhanas, which were an occasional feature of many of the war theatres, reached a level of sophistication which would have impressed on Newmarket Heath: properly railed courses, a tote and a paddock. Less conventionally, there was wrestling on horseback, a mounted tug of war and a mule race.

Chapter 6

Salonika and Gallipoli

Stanley Spencer's painting of the wounded arriving at a dressing station in Macedonia gives as full an acknowledgement of the horses as of the wounded men themselves. If it is acceptable to attribute sympathy to horses, Spencer here unmistakably endows them with this emotion as they stare at the operation going on in front of them.

Spencer's paintings, inspired by the war hospitals he worked at in England and in Macedonia, are intensely precise yet emotional canvases built round the most mundane of practicalities – men and women scrubbing and disinfecting cupboards, filling tea urns, sorting the laundry. But the animals – his tortoises, as well as his mules and horses – have a place in his story of the War, as in no other artist's work. This picture, painted in 1919, was a commission from the War Artists Advisory Committee.

Spencer was one of the celebrated group of Slade students centred round Dora Carrington and Mark Gertler and patronized by Lady Ottoline Morrell in the years leading up to and during the War. He volunteered first to join the Royal Army Medical Corps and was sent to the Beaufort Hospital in Bristol, an experience of unrelenting misery. But then in 1916 he was sent out to Greece, to Smol in Macedonia. The medical services there soon found themselves dealing with the failed British attempt to push Bulgaria out of the War. The attack, which ended in a long stalemate, provoked a stream of casualties to Smol. While in Bristol, Spencer had had neither the time nor the inclination to paint. But then the sudden and unexpected success of a painting he did not even know was being exhibited in London, his voyage to the romanticized classicism of Greece and then the fearful immediacy of the casualties all gave a new impetus to his artistic sensibilities. He told his sister, 'I would not have missed seeing the things I have seen since I left England, for anything', and writing of this painting, he said, 'I felt there was grandeur there. All those wounded men were calm and at peace with everything, so the pain seemed a small thing with them.'

The conditions on the Salonika front were as bad as anywhere in the war – mud as deep as Flanders, humidity, temperatures capable of dropping, as they did in December 1917, from 66° Fahrenheit to 13° of frost in less than a week, accompanied by rain squalls and snow. When the British forces arrived, their animals' coats were unclipped and became soaked; hay was in short supply; almost half of the horses got sand colic; they could not digest the uncrushed barley given to them; and the horse lines offered no protection from wind and weather. Yet they were supposed to haul heavy artillery to the top of the Macedonian hills, as well as the shells and supplies to support it. The route back to the vet hospitals saw lines of twenty or more sick and debilitated horse being led on a single rope.

Travoys Arriving with Wounded at a Dressing Station, Smol, Macedonia, Stanley Spencer. (*Imperial War Museum, London UK/ Bridgeman Images*)

Pack Transport Advancing over Mountainous Country, Robert Blythe. (*Imperial War Museum, London, UK*)

Then the ever resourceful army vets came up with a solution: simply turn the horses loose. And so the area behind the front soon offered the unique sight of hundreds, even thousands, of horses wandering freely over the plain. The forage was poor, but the movement and exercise produced a spectacular improvement in their condition. The vets reported that they became punctual, almost to the minute, in filing back to their own lines at feed times, quite without direction and often at a slow jog trot.

The British and French troops who had been sent to Salonika, after an initial advance, found themselves having to retreat to a defensive line on the Greek border in the most trying conditions. They became utterly dependent on mules. The official history recounts:

> The animals of the divisional train were working as much as eighteen hours a day and travelling on an average twenty miles heavy going, for the roads had by then become almost lakes of mud. Six mules were required normally for each service wagon, and at certain spots ten, or even twelve, were necessary. Much of the movement had to be done at night, including evacuating the sick and wounded.

The mules then had to be converted into pack animals in order to get through the mountain tracks where there were no roads: all the transport had to pass through two difficult gorges with awkward fords. The rearguard suffered especially as heavy rain began to fall. There was to be no rest. Mules which had arrived wearing their pack saddles then had to be reconverted into hauling wagons again by the afternoon. But the retreat had been successfully accomplished, and the front was stabilized.

By the time of the great push up through Bulgaria in 1918, the horses were able to sustain a 500-mile advance in good heart, through dreadful weather and over the roughest roads.

The artist George Denholm Armour, already well past his fiftieth birthday, found himself in charge of the Remount Depot in Salonika. Thirty miles behind the then mainly quiescent front line, he recorded all sorts of sport during these frequent lulls – horse shows in which fully loaded mule squadrons, carrying guns and ammunition, were judged like ballroom dancers, regular polo matches, and General Dowell's pack of rag tag and bobtail beagles, foxhounds and harriers which hunted hares and even a fox or two. Armour wrote:

> I often think these little hounds must hold a record in that they hunted behind the lines in France, possibly Belgium, then Macedonia, and went finally with the Army of the Black Sea to Constantinople.

The Bulgarians, who could see, from their observation balloons, all these entertainments taking place, seem to have regarded them as quaint Britannic diversions, until the Army made the mistake of holding some manoeuvres on the pitch and got bombarded. According to Armour, a Bulgarian plane then came over and dropped a message saying that they had no objection to games, but this military exercise was another thing altogether.

Hunting on the Salonika Front, Lionel Edwards. (*Author*)

Lionel Edwards' painting of hunting at Salonika, puffs of shell smoke in the background in laconic acknowledgement that there was actually a war going on, is an extreme example of the horsemen's implacable determination to indulge in sport wherever and whenever they found a spare moment amid the daily mayhem.

Until the very last months of the war, there was little movement on the Bulgarian Front, though little rest either from raids, artillery, cold, heat and disease. But there was space enough for sport. The hounds in Edwards' picture are perhaps too flattering an echo of Leicestershire's finest. In fact, they had been impressed, at the cost of a King's shilling or so, from local Greek farmers and villagers, and trained by two professional huntsmen from the Old Surrey and the North Cotswold, who happened to find themselves in the ranks of the Scottish Horse.

MFH to the Salonika Hunt was Lieutenant Colonel George Railston. Hacking around behind the trenches in the summer of 1917, he could not resist the invitingly open country along the Struma River and the certainty that there was sport to be had there once the winter closed in. Hence twelve couple of hounds, mongrel but of suitable temperament, were acquired, and by the time of the first frosts they were ready for an inaugural meet. It is recorded that the Corps Commander, Sir Charles Briggs, and five other Generals were among the 125 mounted followers who arrived in good time for drinks and refreshment before the field set off.

The hunt met throughout that winter of 1917/18, occasionally interrupted by sporadic shelling. Dismay was caused when Molyneux, the Old Surrey professional, hot on the heels of the hounds as they followed their quarry into no-man's-land, insouciantly put his pony at a new barbed wire fence five feet high and eight feet wide – and simply flew over it. The local commander enquired how it was supposed to stop Bulgarians, when it had not outfaced a pony.

Come the summer, and the irrepressible Lieutenant Colonel Railston knew that what chaps did in the balmier months was, of course, play polo. His peregrinations behind the barbed wire had permitted him to identify a flat patch of sandy soil of sufficient dimensions for a proper chukka. Reeds and long grass had to be dealt with first, and then there was the problem of the ponies. Balls and sticks had already made it to base, and they were easily purloined. But only a few of the Scottish Horse's mounts showed any aptitude, and the squad had to be made up with local ponies of the requisite agility.

Railston set about schooling and coaching his team until he felt confident enough to challenge the adjoining Surrey Yeomanry, who boasted some experienced old polo men amongst their ranks. A time was fixed, and the contestants were instructed to make their way individually by different routes to the field, which was well within range of the Bulgarian artillery. The game duly took place, and Railston and his men were rewarded with an unlooked-for victory.

After polo, custom requires tea, and the Colonel did not fail them. A pack horse had been loaded with the necessary refreshments and sent forward. Unfortunately, the Bulgarians had woken up to strange activity in the opposing lines, and a shower of shrapnel broke up the tea party, mercifully with no injury to man or horse. In the ensuing weeks polo continued, but tea was abandoned.

In the spring of 1915 the politicians and strategists in Whitehall devised a plan to attack the underbelly of the Turkish enemy. Thus British, Australian, New Zealand and Indian troops found themselves thrown into what became the debacle of Gallipoli. It was to be the scene of repeated acts of gallant heroism, extremes of heat and cold, dreadful casualty figures and, finally, withdrawal and retreat.

Gallipoli is a peninsula on the west coast of Turkey, offering cliffs, inlets and narrow beaches to an invader. And in 1915 it was provided with considerable Turkish defences. In its 400 pages, the official history of the calamitous Gallipoli campaign makes no mention of the horses. Yet at one point there were more than 40,000 horses, mules and donkeys crammed under the cliffs and mustered on the constricted beaches of the peninsula.

Transported the 800 sea miles from Egypt along with the troops, each animal had to be disembarked by being slung out on to small boats, for there were no harbours, and then brought ashore to the beaches. There were only a handful of horse lighters, most carrying twenty or so animals each although a few took up to seventy, so the vast majority of animals had to be hauled in slings over the ships' sides and deposited on to small rafts and boats to get them ashore. The gun horses then had to haul first the guns, then the ammunition, the water barrels and the stores up through the sand under steady Turkish artillery fire. The men soon discovered that the only way to protect the horse lines was to burrow into the cliffs and carve out standings which could offer protection from the sporadic shelling.

These tortuous processes, under enemy fire almost from the start, meant that there was a limit to the numbers of horses and mules that could be landed. A gun team, once landed, would have to return repeatedly to the shore to haul more guns up from the beach and to bring up ammunition, rations, forage and supplies, under constant shell fire. No plans had been made for where to keep the horses or how to water them. Water had to be brought in by lighter for the horses as for the men. The Turks soon realized that dust clouds meant horses on the move, and shelled them accordingly. Watering at night became the only option.

The tribulations escalated. Hay could not be fed on the ground, for it either blew away or the horses absorbed sand with it and went down with sand colic. But there were not enough hay nets. The Army had sent out heavy horseshoes, which were another burden to the animals. Above all, there was the shelling. One shell alone at Cape Helles took out eighteen horses. The veterinary officers found themselves confined to dugouts, emerging in intervals between the shells to shoot the seriously wounded cases. On one occasion Lieutenant C.M. Stuart reported having to shoot eighty hopelessly wounded animals.

Shoeing under Difficulties, Thomas Dugdale. (*Imperial War Museum, London, UK*)

Then there was the problem of what to do with the carcases. At first they tried digging mass graves. Men returning from the firing lines were roped in, but the sand made the exercise almost futile, and suitable sites were scarce. Then they tried towing the carcases out to sea, hoping the currents would take them away. But most of them drifted back to shore, adding to the health hazards from the flies on the piles of horse dung. Finally, the Navy was persuaded to take the dead mules and horses further out, where they were cut open, weighted with stones and thrown overboard. The sailors faced with this macabre task continually had to cope with danger from under the surface – and more than once the upturned hoofs of dead horses in the water were mistaken for the periscopes of Turkish submarines. The submarines were no idle threat, either. His Majesty's ship *Marquette* went down off the Gallipoli coast in October 1915 and all 541 horses on board were lost along with her crew.

Unique privations confronted the horses and the horsemen at Gallipoli. The horses were permitted just one watering session each day, under cover of darkness. Their droppings soon became intensive fly-breeding factories. The horses needed head fringes to help protect them both from the flies and the sun. Eventually, supplies came from the Blue Cross charity. Yet the horsemen, forced to cope with conditions of extreme heat and, before the whole sorry venture ended, extreme cold, were remarkably successful in keeping their animals in good condition. Diseases like glanders, so prevalent in other theatres of war, were kept at bay. Even after several months of demanding labour, hauling guns and supplies, most of the horses kept their condition.

The Gallipoli campaign began in the April of 1915 and lasted into the following New Year. After the initial landings there were gallant attempts to gain the higher ground beyond the beaches and to overcome some of the fortified Turkish positions. These attacks, by the British, French, Australian, New Zealand and Indian troops, all required very large quantities of ammunition and stores to be brought up to the jump-off positions. The horses, mules and donkeys bore most of the weight of this work, moving almost always at night. Eventually, after months of desperate fighting, the French and British agreed to withdraw and employ their resources across the other side of the Aegean in the Salonika campaign against the Bulgarians.

There had been some disastrous times. The supply beaches were constantly shelled. The Indian Transport Corps lost a third of their animals – more than 800 horses – before the withdrawal. But throughout the eight months of the Gallipoli venture, the horsemen were extraordinarily successful in keeping their charges alive and working. The weekly reports of losses rarely exceeded one or two per cent. And even after fierce storms and cold in the November and December of 1915, most of the horses returning to Egypt were soon restored to active service condition.

When the doomed adventure of Gallipoli finally ended, the Allied armies showed extraordinary tenacity and organization in extracting themselves from Gallipoli under continuous harassment from the Turks. More than 4,000 animals were lifted on board at the Suvla and Anzac beaches, with only 263 being lost. At Cape Helles they lost more than 900 in the eleven days of the evacuation, but still managed to rescue more than 3,000 and take them the 800 miles back to Egypt.

One affecting picture, beneath the wintry Turkish hills, with its implication of a long and painful trek already endured and more to come, is actually of a Royal Navy stretcher party, detached, as many were, for battle duty on land. One must assume the horse was somehow commandeered. The horse-borne stretcher was one of the innumerable devices which the troops contrived to recover their wounded, both human and equine. Evacuating the wounded was a constant challenge, whether it was, like Siegfried Sassoon, simply trying to haul men out of shell holes by rope, or using stretchers, carts and wagons or, as was the case by the end of the war, sophisticated covered horse-drawn ambulances.

This painting is by Jan Gordon. He and his wife Cora were popular travel writers and artists, chronicling a series of joys and misadventures in the Balkans and elsewhere before the War. Jan was recruited into the Royal Navy as an official artist and produced a devastating series of paintings of the mayhem of injured and wounded sailors aboard one of the Navy's battleships. His attachment to the medical services eventually found him ashore in the campaign against the Turks.

Gordon had previously helped fellow artist Norman Wilkinson to develop the almost Cubist-style 'Dazzle' camouflage system. Its angular shapes and varied shadows were adopted by most Navy ships by the end of the war, and Gordon became a leading theorist of what was one of the more effective artistic contributions to the war effort.

RN Armoured Car Squadron: Transport of Wounded on the Turkish Front, Jan Gordon. (*Imperial War Museum, London, UK*)

Chapter 7

Around the World

The painted record is vivid testimony that the First War truly was a World War, with action in Asia and across Africa as well as in Europe and the Middle East, sometimes in areas where the horses were particularly vulnerable to disease. But it is enemy action which has killed Captain Learoyd's horse in George Derville Rowlandson's picture. Private Charles Hull is saving his officer's life, for which he won the VC. The incident took place at Hafiz Kor, in one of the truly forgotten theatres, the North West frontier of India.

The Turks and German agents had stirred up the tribes on the frontier, and Hull and Learoyd belonged to the 21st Lancers, who had been sent up in 1915 to deal with the trouble. Hull, who had been a postman in Harrogate in Yorkshire, was a shoeing smith with the Lancers. When Learoyd's horse was shot from under him, though there was constant firing from tribesmen who were very close, Hull dashed forward on his horse and hauled the officer up behind him. They galloped off to safety. Hull only got home in 1919, after nine years away, to receive a civic welcome and the thanks of Captain Learoyd's parents. Sadly, by then the Captain had succumbed to influenza and pneumonia in India and never made it home himself.

After more than a century of frontier war in India, the military were confident that their horses were bred and reared for the massive landscapes of the Himalayas and the mountain passes. But in 1915 the army vets were struggling with a truly severe outbreak of equine flu, which affected almost every horse in the military establishments across India. At the same time mules and ponies were being shipped in, not only from Tibet and Persia, but from as far away as the Argentine, bringing with them an array of afflictions and diseases with which the Indian vets were not familiar. More than half the ponies were suffering from mange and a disease called *surra*. It often took months to restore them to serviceable health.

Hardly had the tribesmen been subdued when another old enemy emerged, Russia. This time, after the 1917 revolutions, there was almost a panic over the possibility of Bolshevik incursions, and a force was sent back to the Afghanistan frontier. But the imported diseases had not been conquered, and it was said that one could trace the force's track across the desert to Saindak by following the skeletons of abandoned Army animals, camels as well as horses.

Before the revolutions, of course, the Russians had been heavily engaged on the Allies' side against both the German and Austrian armies. Nikolai Borisov's picture of a Russian cavalry assault on German guns conveys the intensity of the hand-to-hand fighting in which most cavalry charges ended. The Russians had more than thirty cavalry divisions when the war started. But in the first great battle of the Eastern front at Tannenberg in August 1914, the

Private C. Hull Saving the Life of Captain G.E.D. Learoyd, under Fire, George Derville Rowlandson. (Private Collection/ The Stapleton Collection/ Bridgeman Images)

Germans, under Hindenburg and Ludendorff, in inflicting an almost decisive defeat on the Russians, managed to destroy almost completely the mounted Don Cossacks. The Germans continued to use their own cavalry on the eastern front against the Russians, with some success, long after they had withdrawn cavalry in the West.

The picture by Sydney Carline, brother of Richard, is unusual, if not unique. Most of his paintings were of aerial combat and life in the Royal Flying Corps and Royal Air Force. Moreover, it was painted in one of the forgotten theatres of the First World War, the Italian front – these days perhaps only remembered for Ernest Hemingway's account of the fighting there in *A Farewell to Arms*.

Carline, another graduate of the Slade in its brilliant pre-war manifestation, was one of the earliest pilots in the Royal Flying Corps. He was shot down over the Somme in 1916 and wounded. But he recovered and was sent to fly the legendary Sopwith Camel fighter planes in Italy. The British and the French had been concerned to help prop up their Italian allies against the Austrians after the calamitous defeat at Caporetto to the north of Venice in 1917.

The painting shows the horse-drawn artillery crowded in the streets of Vicenza. These troops, along with Carline and his fellow fighter pilots, were to prove crucial, first in halting the Austrian advance and then pushing them back over the Alps to final capitulation in October 1918, in what has been described as one of the most exemplary tactical achievements of the entire war.

The British delivered five divisions and 26,000 artillery horses, pack mules and even cavalry, by train through France to the Italian front. The mules and artillery horses immediately found themselves taking guns and ammunition up to the front and building up for the big offensive against the Austrians on the Piave River. The British cavalry had to wait until the final attack of late October 1918, which overwhelmed the enemy. Sweeping on ahead of the infantry, as the cavalry had imagined themselves doing throughout the war, in pursuit of a disintegrating army, they rounded up thousands of prisoners.

In South Africa, where the Boer war had ended scarcely a decade earlier, there was almost immediately a rebellion by Boer officers who favoured Germany. Indeed, Manie Maritz, who became the principal leader of the revolt, got himself appointed a full German Army general within the month. Both the South African government of Louis Botha and the rebels realized that the mounted tactics which had been refined so sharply during the Boer War might well prove crucial again. Consequently, there was a rush to acquire horses. There had been only 8,000 military horses left in South Africa in the summer of 1914, but by the time the rebels were defeated there were 160,000. The horsemen were immediately required to make major marches – one across 400 miles of desert from Kimberley – and at the same time take maximum precautions against diseases such as anthrax which were rife in the area.

There was high tension in some of the military camps, because no one knew how many officers and troops would go over to the rebels. The government vets in Uppington camp found themselves organizing sentries armed with Maxim machine guns to guard their horse

The Russian Cavalry Charging the German Artillery in 1915, Nikolai Borisov. (State Central Artillery Museum, St Petersburg, Russia/ Bridgeman Images)

French Artillery Passing British Artillery in a village near Vicenza, 7 April 1918, Sydney Carline. (*Imperial War Museum, London, UK*)

lines against a surprise coup. They were relieved when the Natal Light Horse and Enslin's Horse arrived – though they themselves brought plenty of work for the vets, with sore backs from hasty tacking up and ill-fitting saddles. They were supposed to bring a significant number of pack donkeys, but most, being too young for the job, had died en route. The rest were in very poor condition.

There then ensued more or less a re-run of the Boer war fighting. The rebel commandos ranged around on their horses, preventing the government animals being put out to graze and cutting off the supply of forage through the railroad. The government horses declined into a woeful condition. But after two abortive rebel attacks on Uppington, help arrived in the shape of the South African 4th Mounted Brigade, and the rebellion collapsed. One of the rebel leaders, General Kemp, in an attempt to escape to German South West Africa, took 800 men and their horses on a 1,100-kilometre trek across the Kalahari desert. Only 300 men made it, and almost none of the horses.

Meanwhile, the South Africans set about capturing German South West Africa. Again, horses were crucial. The animals were embarked on a small fleet of civilian ships and sailed round to Walvis Bay. The South Africans found out for themselves the problems of transporting horses by ship which afflicted other theatres of the war – the animals were packed so tightly (some even in ship's corridors) that they sometimes could not be watered, and food was either insufficient or consisted of mealies, which produced colic. But the Army still managed to land 43,000 animals in two months at Walvis Bay. Ashore, there was not enough shelter or hard standing, and even water was in short supply. Despite three months of recuperation before the South Africans launched their advance against the German forces, many of the horses remained in quite poor condition.

The South West Africa campaign was almost totally dependent on horses. It was to end after three months in a German surrender. But victory brought perhaps the worst calamity of the Great War anywhere for the horses and mules. The advance had been tough enough, some of the units covering 40 miles in a day during a 250-mile trek. Lack of water and forage produced utter exhaustion, with hundreds of horses and mules being simply abandoned along the way, in the hope that they would be picked up by the support veterinary services. By the time of the surrender, there were about 60,000 government animals, to which were added a large number taken over from the defeated Germans. The volatile political situation in Cape Town meant that the South African government was anxious to get the troops home as quickly as possible. They were encouraged to use empty railway cars and other transport to get themselves home, but little thought was given to how to deal with the horses and transport animals. An official report concluded:

It was after the declaration of the Peace that the greatest loss and harm befell the animals. It is impossible to describe the state of the animals on their return from the north of German South West Africa. It was a case of survival of the fittest. Riders left their horses anywhere on the veldt.

Debilitated as they were, they were slowly gathered in until there were more than 60,000 animals in half a dozen remount camps set up along the railway line. At the time, there were 15,000 tons of forage and food stored at the dockside at Walvis Bay. But a complete failure of organization meant that almost none of it reached the starving horses. At first the remount officers contemplated trying to trek the animals back to South Africa. But it was 700 miles or more over the barest of ground. Several attempts were made to herd the horses down the coast towards Walvis, and the route became strewn with carcases. The official report ended:

> During the four months after the cessation of hostilities, several thousand animals died from starvation or were shot, and thousands more reduced to an extremely low condition.

When the time came to take on the Germans in East Africa – modern Tanzania – the South Africans were faced with an entirely different problem. The campaign was to extend from the slopes of Kilimanjaro down to low-lying areas which were known to be among the most deadly places on earth for horses, and indeed cattle and other beasts. Yet mounted troops were the only way of conducting effective warfare. The German commander Naumann led the South Africans a merry dance through mountains and thick lowland bush and across rivers and lakes for more than a thousand miles.

Both sides understood the lethal nature of these tropical diseases and, indeed, where they were likely to infect the horses. In the early part of the campaign the South African commanders managed to keep their mounted troops away from areas, beside rivers and in the low country, where the tsetse fly and the mosquito were to be found in abundance. But it was in the East African campaign that disease itself became a weapon of war. The German commander-in-chief, under pressure and retiring towards the coast, took regular advice from his veterinary officer as to where the most deadly locations for animals were. He then placed his infantry to entice the South Africans down a route which led to a town called Morogoro. South African vets later conceded that he had brought about the death of 12,000 horses and mules this way, in less than four months. Hardly any horses survived.

These risks were known to the South African commanders. Indeed, they were warned that equine loss could well reach 100 per cent. But they took the view that victory required them to enter these lethal zones. By the end of the campaign 31,000 horses had been engaged, of which only 800 survived; fewer than 900 mules lived out of 33,000; and just 1,400 donkeys out of 34,000. The main killer was African horse sickness – still an unresolved problem in the present day – and the fly-borne disease trypanosomiasis. There were already some vaccines being developed and delivered, and it was known that the depredations of the tsetse fly could be prevented by feeding horses a tablet of arsenic every day. The problem was to persuade the horsemen to do this effectively by crushing the tablets in the feed, not just leaving them to be rejected at the bottom of the bucket. In fact, by the time of the Great War, the numbers of knowledgeable South African horsemen who had made the Boer commandos so effective

Keeping its Place in the Kilimanjaro Column: 13-pounder Gun Treks on Three Wheels and a Tree Trunk, English School. (*Private Collection/ The Stapleton Collection/ Bridgeman Images*)

only a decade or so earlier had greatly diminished. Yet it was horsemen who were now needed. One mounted officer lamented in 1915: 'It is less difficult to find a man who can clean a sparking plug than one who can adjust a saddle or bridle in a workmanlike fashion.'

Camouflaged behind the glamour of the cavalry horses and the magnificence of the Percherons and Shires, the British Army's mules drew scant attention and had a reputation for recalcitrance. But they were often the beasts of last resort when it came to moving difficult loads or tackling almost impassable roads.

George Armour, with his Salonika experience, spoke of their 'wonderful qualities as draught animals' and told how his men took great pride in their achievements. He describes one occasion on the Bulgarian front when a big gun got bogged down and double teams of horses could not move it. The commanding officer of a nearby squadron was the most enthusiastic of mule men and he sent down a team of six of his prize grey mules. The gun was rescued in short order.

Armour asserts as common knowledge that mules are more intelligent than horses. Like all animals, he says, they respond to good food and treatment but, at a pinch, they can exist where a horse would die and work under conditions where he would be useless. As with horses, the principal hazard to mules in desert conditions was sand colic. It was often fatal, and Armour records seeing 70lb of sand found in the guts of a dead mule.

The experience of the War in every theatre led the Army vets to form the warmest appreciation of the mule's merits. Whether transported by land or sea, mules had a mortality rate less than half that of horses, and their resistance to disease was much higher. Moreover, they subsisted on only three quarters of the rations of a horse – a significant fact or at a time when the forage requirements of horses was already becoming a stick which the motor men were using to beat the horsemen.

The mule was, in fact, crucial to the Allied effort. There were more than 40,000 in use on the Salonika front, more than 50,000 in Egypt and Mesopotamia. Even on the Western Front in France and Flanders, nearly a third of the transport and haulage animals, more than 90,000, were mules.

In the spring of 1918, the Austrians had tried to take the initiative against the Italians in the mountains around Piave. The plateau around which much of the fighting occurred was more than 4,000 feet up. Here the mules proved invaluable. They took 200lb packs of ammunition the 20 miles up from the plains in three or four hours on tracks which horses could not manage. At the height of the Austrian offensive, a group of twenty mules were recorded as working eighteen hours a day for eight consecutive days, carrying 500 gallons of water every day and carting 600 rolls of barbed wire, as well as mortars and ammunition. At night they were harassed by shell and small arms fire – all this on diminished rations and, sometimes, twelve hours or more without water.

Perhaps the only place where the mule was found wanting was the Russian front around Archangel. The British and French took nearly a thousand mules – though almost no horses – northward in 1918 and 1919 to aid the Whites in the Russian Civil War, but soon found

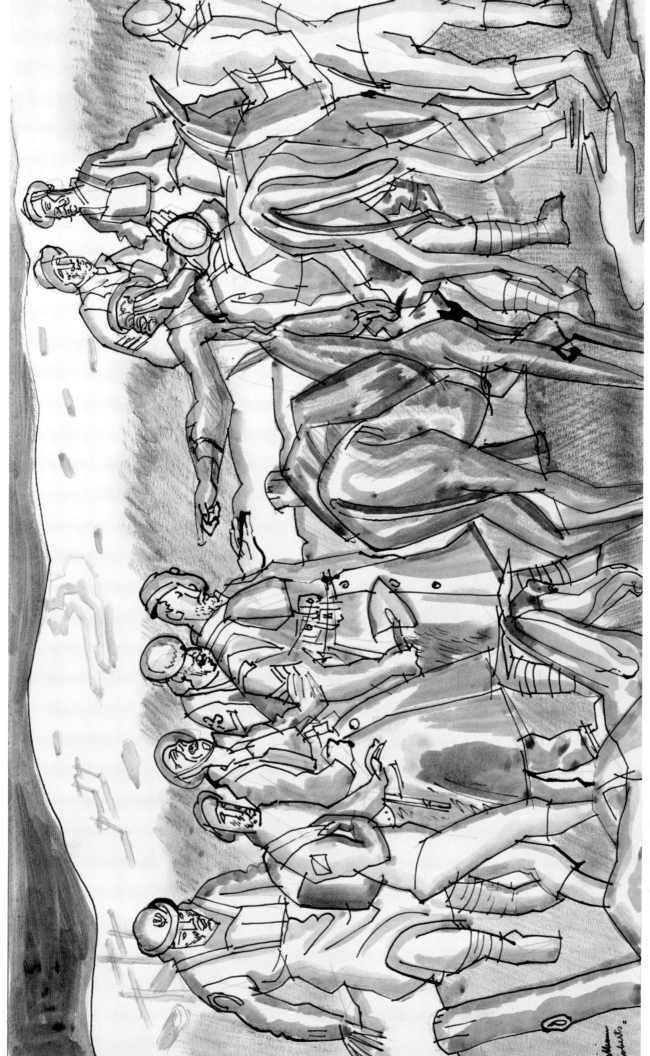

Pack Mules, William Roberts. (*Imperial War Museum, London, UK*)

that the mules could not really cope with the rivers and the boggy terrain. It was the native Russian pony which could pick its way through the soft spots; and when it came to crossing rivers, the Russian pony, load and all, would happily plunge in and swim across, whereas the mules on more than one occasion managed to drown themselves and their riders.

If the mule was the unsung hero, the donkeys were the choir behind the curtain. Even the artists seemed to regard them as worthy only of filling in the background of camp scenes. Yet they proved critical in many theatres of the War. When the big push was being planned out of Egypt in 1917 up to Palestine, the logistic calculations suggested that there was nothing like enough camel and horse transport. So the Army set about buying donkeys. In just three months they bought more than 12,000 donkeys from local Egyptians. The Army found their new purchases to be notably satisfactory. A report read:

> They were an excellent lot of animals, remarkably uniform in size, free from lameness and vice, and repeatedly proved their worth during the operations in the Judaean hills.

The main problem was getting them shod for the long trek ahead. Somehow the Remount depot managed to corral enough blacksmiths to fit all 12,000 with the local type of shoe, which, unfortunately, later proved inadequate in the mountains and had to be exchanged for Army shoes. They were issued with eye fringes to keep off the flies and checked for mange and other diseases. Then they were ready for service.

The donkeys were organized into companies of 200, mainly looked after by locally recruited Egyptians. The sudden change from the hot flatlands of Egypt to the mountains did indeed prove challenging. Two hundred donkeys died, but the rest rapidly acclimatized and remained a valuable element in the victorious campaign all the way to Damascus, though 500 more of them were killed in action or lost in the last few months of the desert war.

Donkeys were also used in East Africa, where more than 30,000 died of disease in the fetid lowlands of Tanganyika. Only a handful – just thirty – went to Gallipoli. The Germans and their allies in Eastern Europe, however, found themselves accepting that in Bulgaria donkeys were a prime form of basic transport, and thousands were recruited into the supply chain.

With all the troops two animals became firm favourites – the Abyssinian horse and mule. There were only about a thousand of these mules, brought down through Kenya and standing only twelve or thirteen hands high, but it was reported:

> They have wonderful powers of endurance. Their capacity for work under war conditions with scarce rations made them very popular with the East African Expeditionary Force. As pack mules for hilly country or harness mules for light draught, they have few equals. They are easily broken to saddle and are capable of carrying a trooper with his full equipment great distances without showing fatigue.

Sadly, the military authorities could not be persuaded to splash out and import a lot more of them.

The British were to become enamoured of a number of the local pony and horse breeds they came across in the War. The ultimately futile adventure up to Archangel in Russia to try and help the White Russians at least produced an admiring acquaintance with the little Russian pony. 'The Russian pony is a wonderful little animal,' an officer reported, 'varying from 12 to 13.2 hands. They are shabby, long coated and small. The distance they are able to cover when drawing a sleigh is marvellous.' This was after British mules and cobs were proving a dismal failure in the snow.

Chapter 8

The Americans

The renown of conquest is often shared by the great commanders with their horses. Jan van Chelminski's portrait of General Pershing riding Kidron is in the grand tradition.

The Duke of Wellington rode Copenhagen. Napoleon had more than a hundred known mounts but is most famously portrayed on the grey Marengo. In 1945 General MacArthur planned to flaunt American triumph by riding the Japanese Emperor's white charger through defeated Tokyo. General Allenby, by contrast, pointedly dismounted and walked through the Jaffa Gate to announce, with planned diffidence, the British capture of Jerusalem. Only twenty years earlier, the Kaiser had ridden through that same gate to assert his alliance with the Turks.

But Kidron was, for a time, the most famous of them all. The whole of America had seen General John J. Pershing in the newsreels riding him after Germany's collapse in 1918. They had seen him at the forefront of the Allied victory parade down the Champs-Elysées in Paris. They had seen the General and Kidron given the most tumultuous welcome in Manhattan as the American Expeditionary Force returned victorious from Europe and passed under the Victory Arch. And they made sure that their equine hero had the finest of retirements at Front Royal military base in Virginia. Today, his bones can still be seen at the American Museum of Natural History in Washington.

Chelminski was Polish-born, but naturalized British. He had made his name with expansive historical pictures, including one of Napoleon and Marengo, before marrying the daughter of New York art dealer Ronald Knoedler and finding an American clientele.

General John J. Pershing himself was the epitome of the American military hero. He had made his name as a young officer leading an impossibly brave assault on San Juan Hill in the Spanish-American War of 1898. Even as the Great War was developing in Europe, he had been despatched in 1915 by President Wilson to confound, and if possible to capture, Pancho Villa, the Mexican bandit and revolutionary general, who had dared to make a flamboyant raid across the US border and plunder Columbus, New Mexico.

When the Americans, provoked by German submarine attacks on their shipping and the insistent pleas from Britain to join the defence of democracy, finally joined the war in 1917, it was Pershing whom the President selected to lead the American force on the Western Front. The very first contingent of just sixty-seven men who landed in France with Pershing in June 1917 included thirty-one members of the 2nd Cavalry regiment.

When the United States finally decided to join the War, the administration had reacted with extraordinary speed and decisiveness. An immediate and huge expansion of the Navy was

General Pershing, Jan van Chelminski. (*Gavin Graham Gallery, London, UK/ Bridgeman Images*)

authorized, including four new battleships, as well as an intense drive for aircraft production. But it was also decided that a key element of the American Expeditionary Force should be a cavalry regiment. And with commendable imagination the authorities immediately decided to commission eight official American war artists.

The dispatch of cavalry was the result of careful monitoring by the Americans of what had been happening on the Western Front. They knew that horsemen had shown their mobility was valuable in conditions where mechanical transport could not progress. They knew that communications could best be safely transmitted by horsemen – indeed Pershing kept half a dozen of the 2nd's troopers permanently with him. They knew that the Allies still felt that cavalry could have a role in exploiting breakthroughs and victories.

But the Americans had also studied seriously how the cavalry should be armed. Sabres were relegated to ceremonial duty only, and the 2nd were given a semi-automatic pistol, the M1911 .45. This was intended for mounted action, but they also carried the M1903 bolt-action rifle for dismounted use. They were the only American soldiers to carry more than one firearm.

The cavalry found their equestrian expertise was in demand in a variety of areas. Some were drafted in to help gassed and wounded French Army horses, including great Percherons and even a Spanish pony, and return them to service. But then they were ordered to join the big American push of September 1918, first for reconnaissance and then to move into the open country around Nonsard. This produced their first serious encounter, when they ran into a large German formation gathering to retreat.

One of the 2nd Cavalry units immediately charged. But they were confounded by German machine gun fire, with a number of the horses simply bolting. The events of that day showed up some dangerous gaps in the Regiment's armoury. Some horses were needed specifically to carry additional ammunition (it had simply run out). They needed machine guns with them. And the Cavalry's officers felt a number of their men should carry hand grenades. There was also to be a new emphasis on horse care, for the exertions of just a month of action in France had rendered almost half the horses unfit for service.

George Matthews Harding was one of the first American war artists to get to France. He wrote feelingly in his diary of 'the screech of the guns, the whine of the shells as they go over' and the calm of the troops. Harding, a Philadelphia man, had already travelled the South Seas, been shipwrecked off Labrador and established a reputation as a painter of the wild and the adventurous. He was fascinated by the endless bustle of life in the lines. His painting *Army Camp 1917* shows the energetic melange of horse and soldier. *Traffic to Mont St Père* has American troopers jostling past German prisoners being sent to the rear.

Another of the official artists, Wallace Morgan, a New Yorker who had been with *Colliers* magazine and who had crossed America for them chronicling ordinary life, found himself close up to the front in the final advances. His drawing *Infantry and Tanks Advancing 1918* shows how the officers still found they needed to be mounted, to move easily around the battlefields.

US Cavalry Machine Gun Troop Showing Vickers-Maxim Watch Cooled Machine Guns, American School. (Private Collection/ © Galerie Bilderwelt/ Bridgeman Images)

Army Camp 1917, George Matthews Harding. (*Courtesy of the Army Art Collection, US Army Center of Military History*)

Traffic to Mont St Père, George Matthews Harding (Armed Forces History Division, National Museum of American History, Smithsonian Institution, USA) Matthews Harding, Mont St Pere

Infantry and Tanks Advancing 1918, Wallace Morgan (Armed Forces History Division, National Museum of American History, Smithsonian Institution, USA) Morgan, Infantry

General Pershing had been determined, at first, that the Americans should retain independence of command. But in the tense days of the Kaiser's spring offensive in 1918, and then in the relentless summer pressure on the Germans, Pershing joined in the overall strategy which produced the final disintegration of the German war effort. Pershing was a commander who believed in being up with his fighting troops. And, almost invariably, Kidron was there too.

Chapter 9

The Home Front

From the first great sweep of horse conscription in August 1914, there was immediate and enduring concern about how the farms were to be worked. There was, after all, a harvest to be gathered within just a week or two; and the farms were almost totally dependent on horses. In the East Riding of Yorkshire, for example, government censuses in the years up to 1913 had shown 40,000 horses working more than 750,000 acres. No tractors were recorded working in the fields. A precise and longstanding structure of labour – entirely male – sustained these enterprises. Men were taken on at the hiring fairs in the country towns and committed to staying on the farm a full year. The foreman was in overall charge, but it was the waggoner who effectively organized the horse lads and set the tasks of the day.

The women, virtually without exception, worked in service indoors, providing not only for the families but also for the farmhands who lived in the massive farm houses which, to this day, can be seen on the Yorkshire Wolds. Harvest was the only time that women were seen in the fields.

When war came, however, the women were rapidly pressed into service. Cecil Aldin's picture of a Land Girl ploughing was commissioned to memorialize the efforts of the quarter of a million women who joined the Women's Land Army, a formal national service institution, founded by Dame Meriel Talbot in early 1917.

The painting has a primitive quality, with the pair of grey horses and the simple plough being guided by the lone figure of the plough girl. The tasks facing the Land Girls were dauntingly demanding, even by the standards of 1914. For not only had the farms of Britain been denuded of men – the estimate was that half the agricultural workers on the Yorkshire Wolds had gone to the war – but also the machinery which had started to appear on the farms in the first decade of the century was starved of fuel and spare parts. The women who, perforce, had to take over much of the men's work had to endure real hard labour.

In the first two years of the war, farmers and landowners largely had to make shift for themselves, with many of the women transferring from domestic service to the open fields.

Meriel Talbot's initiative gave organization and direction to Government policy on using women in every possible way to aid the war effort – at the same time, the munitions factories were being taken over and worked by women, the 'munitionettes' – at a time when the depredations of German submarines were producing alarming shortfalls in food and oil.

The Land Army was launched in the January, with the British Board of Agriculture establishing a Women's Section. The women were given a uniform and some initial training at an agricultural college; and an informal officer class soon emerged from the better educated

A Land Girl Ploughing, Cecil Aldin. (Imperial War Museum, London, UK)

among them. Every county had a Women's War Agricultural Committee, which appointed village registrars in every community. Their job was to discover the farmers' requirements and find the women workers with the necessary skills. By 1918 there were 260,000 women on the Land Army registers.

Cecil Aldin, a devoted hunting man, had been one of the people entrusted with gathering in horses for the war in the first days of August 1914. He had also that year become Master of the South Berks Foxhounds and had the doleful task of seeing the hunt's own horses despatched to the War. Already at forty-four a celebrated painter of hunting and horses, Aldin found himself appointed a captain in the Army, in charge of the Remount depots in Berkshire. There were often three hundred or more horses on his own property in Purley, and thousands to look after around the county. With the shortage of skilled horsemen, Aldin was the pioneer in recruiting women into the Remount depots. Soon there were depots, like Russley Park, entirely run by women. Their job was to take horses which arrived from many parts of the world, as well as local acquisitions, and school them for the various tasks the Army required – gun horses, heavy draught work, riding horses and cavalry chargers. Aldin encouraged his friend Alfred Munnings to come and join the Remount depot, where he turned out to be a most useful hand at treating horse ailments before he was taken away to become an official war artist. Aldin himself suffered the loss of his only son Dudley, who was killed in Flanders in 1916. It fell to Lucy Kemp-Welch to create the paintings of the women at the Remount depots.

The war demanded huge amounts of forage, hay and feed corn for the war horses. The Government launched a Forage Corps, as part of the Service Corps, which soon encompassed 6,000 women tasked solely with keeping the Army's horses fed. As the War implacably continued, the Government became ever more concerned with food supplies both at home and in France. There were instructions to plough up more and more grassland and open up uncultivated areas, so that by the end of the War the farmed land of Britain had increased by more than a quarter.

The new Pathé Animated Gazette newsreels showed all sorts of devices of varying usefulness and absurdity designed to meet the crisis – including an elephant ploughing, with a land girl guiding it and leaving an impeccably straight-looking furrow. The elephant then turned its trunk to tossing sheaves on to a hay cart and even to pumping the water troughs.

The Waggoners memorial outside the gates of Sledmere House in East Yorkshire is perhaps the most intriguing of works of remembrance. It honours the recruitment of more than a thousand of the East Riding's horsemen into the Army during the Great War. The sculptor is Carlo Magnoni. It is decorated with the most grotesque renderings of German troops, intent, it would seem, on rape and pillage. Bayonets, lowering scuttle helmets and bared fangs ensure there can be no doubt about the nature of the evil enemy. One foul Prussian is holding a kneeling woman by her hair.

The Ladies' Army Remount Depot, Russley Park, Wiltshire, 1918, Lucy Kemp-Welch. (*Imperial War Museum, London, UK*)

The Waggoners Memorial. (Author's photo)

Waggoners Memorial, detail. (Author's photo)

The memorial was commissioned by the extraordinary Sir Mark Sykes, who had inherited the baronetcy, along with the burnt-out ruins of Sledmere House, just a year before the War. He was the Sykes of the Sykes-Picot agreement of 1916, which laid the foundations for the carve-up of the Middle East between the British and the French just after the War. By 1919 he was dead, killed by the flu epidemic, only to be disinterred in 2012 by medical researchers who hoped that his lead-lined coffin would have preserved enough of his body to discover if there were clues to the mutating nature of the flu virus.

Even as the ruins of Sledmere were still smouldering in 1911, Mark Sykes' mind was turning towards the likelihood of war on the Continent and what he rightly perceived would be an acute shortage of draught horses for hauling guns and supplies. By 1912 he had received Lord Kitchener's assent to recruit a corps of reservists from the waggoners and ploughmen working the vast arable farms of the Yorkshire Wolds. The process was simple: the men signed their names, were given a sovereign – a seductive amount at a time when they were still being hired for just £20 a year – and that was it. For the next two years they were only required to turn up at Sledmere and confirm their skills by driving a team round an obstacle course at the summer show – until war came.

As the guns of August 1914 sounded, the Waggoners were almost immediately called up. They represented a prime cohort of the skilled horsemen in the East Riding. Simultaneously, the Army Remount service was requisitioning up to a quarter of the 40,000 plough and waggon horses which worked the Wolds. This caused something of a crisis across the unharvested acres, a shortage which was to endure throughout the War.

There is a panel in the memorial showing why these Yorkshire horsemen had such a special appeal to the Army. The Army's guns and supply wagons were nearly all drawn by single poles, rather than the double shafts which were the normal arrangement of most horse-drawn vehicles in Britain. Only in East Yorkshire was the single pole still in dominant use. It requires different skills and different training of horses.

David Hesketh of Burythorpe in Yorkshire, today as knowledgeable as any man on such subjects, explains:

The single pole was much quicker and easier to yoke up. They didn't wear cart saddles. You just hooked them up on either side with the chain from the collar on to the hook behind the swingle tree at the front. They were much more adaptable. You could use almost any size of horse. With shafts, you had to back them in, and then, if you wanted two, put the trace horse on the front. A pole pair was easier to drive. They just set off together. With shafts you have to get the trace horse going with the shaft one. You have to remember the pole carts were cheaper and the lads knew all about them. Some of the lads were farriers and even wheelwrights. The biggest makers of single pole carts were on the Wolds, Sissons of Beswick. And practically every village had a wheelwright who knew how to repair or make new wheels, elm for the axle, oak for the spokes, ash for the rim, and all that skill putting the metal on.

Within days the Waggoners were mustered for uniforms and pay, and within a month they were supporting the British Expeditionary Force in the desperate days of the retreat from Mons. Sykes visited them in late September 1914 near Amiens, under their new title of 20th Division, Army Service Corps.

The Memorial is a narrative of their journey to war. One panel shows men working at home on the land and another is of the men walking off to war, complete with a milestone to York and Driffield. Another sees them receive their pay, and yet another has them on board ship as they join the first BEF units to cross the Channel. Sykes himself made the original drawings for the monument, including the snarling German soldiers grabbing the woman by the hair which in later years drew unavailing protests from the German ambassador in London.

The division served in France throughout the four years of war. Four of the Waggoners were awarded Military Medals.

It was only well into the war, in April 1917, amid fears that the supply to the army might be running out, that the government decided actually to draw up a full census of the number of horses in Great Britain. This showed that in Britain, including Ireland, there were still more than 3,000,000 over and above the 800,000 in Army service, and three quarters of them were still working on the land. But there were also 100,000 employed in London, 25,000 in Liverpool, and 5,000 or more in cities like Sheffield and Birmingham. Their ration was just two pounds of bran a day.

These horses were providing almost all the cartage in the cities, around ten per cent of them, for example, pulling coal wagons. They were still working underground in the coal mines of South Wales and the Midlands – there were 680 pit ponies in the Rhondda valley alone – and between the shafts of the hackney carriages. The railway companies still had more than 40,000 working horses.

From the start of the war there were urgent calls from the Army to recruit horsemen and agricultural workers. At first they were volunteers, but the drain of casualties soon produced conscription, which put great strain on the farmers. Even as late as 1917, another 30,000 farm workers were called up to the colours, at a time when the government was trying to put another two million acres under the plough. There were pleas for the Army to release back, just for the covering and foaling seasons, experienced horsemen from the forces, and this did indeed happen.

There were special prisoner-of-war ploughing camps, where captured Germans were set to work, and horses who became unfit or unwell enough to be up to Army standards were sent back to England and used on the land. For some this was just a period of recuperation before they were sent back to the world of shot and shell. In early 1918 another 22,000 farm workers were called up.

Just as the horse racing fraternity managed to keep some racing going through the war, with the Derby and Oaks being run at Newmarket and the first appearance of girls riding out on the hallowed Heath, so the pedigree horse societies contrived to maintain their key shows, on the grounds that it was in the national interest that the qualities of the best stock, stallions and mares, should be sustained. The Shire Horse Society gratefully accepted an offer to join the Newmarket horse world when an offer came from Messrs Tattersalls to accommodate their annual show in the Park Paddocks sales ring. The Society's Gold Cup was duly presented by Lord and Lady Middleton to Mr T. Forshaw's stallion Rickford Coming King. The best three year old, Speckington Victor Chief, was led in by a uniformed soldier.

At the sales the best Shire stock, working geldings, were fetching £100 or more. One buyer acquired 120 for the Army, not one of which was recorded as making it safely back to England.

Chapter 10

The End of the War

It was on the Bulgarian front that the fighting first ended – and the Army had to face up to disposing of 25,000 horses and mules. With commendable enterprise, it was arranged that notices that the horses were for sale should be read out in every church in Greece, and in Romania too.

The Salonika remount base soon found itself playing host to purchasers from as far away as Crete, to hillmen attired in coats of many colours, and many sleeves as well, to Romanian army officers in scarlet breeches and gold lace, and above all to Greek government officials, who ended up buying 10,000 animals. All this competition allowed the British to set what they judged to be fair prices – and stick to them. All but animals over the age of sixteen were sold. The old horses were shot. Thus was set a pattern which was to be followed in all the theatres, despite the doleful thoughts of the horsemen. 'It was a very distasteful thing to have to sell these animals into the slavery which would inevitably be their fate,' wrote the remount depot commander.

Throughout the War, there was constant fretting about what to do with dead animals or those which had become, as the categorization had it, 'unserviceable'. Close to the front line the dead were skinned – there was a good market for the hides back in England – and then buried as best as could be. The Army vets soon found, however, that they could sell animals to local farmers and that there was an eager market for horseflesh in Paris for human consumption.

The British were less keen on horse steaks and mule mince, so at first any spare meat was given to prisoners of war and to the multinational cohorts of the labour brigades. But there was then instituted a serious campaign to persuade the British man in the street that horse meat was a significant and acceptable alternative to the beef that had vanished from the shops. After various conferences with local butchers it was decided that the citizens of London and Liverpool should have the privilege of becoming the first horseflesh tasters.

They seem to have taken to it well enough, with two hundred horses a week being consumed, although the horseflesh gourmets faded away after the war's end.

The French and Belgian butchers needed no persuading to take on the surplus horsemeat. More than 25,000 horses went to Paris butchers alone. Nearly 40,000 hides were shipped back to England in the last year of the war. After the Armistice, more than 150,000 animals were sold in France, with 30,000 of them going to the butchers. Of the gallant horses which had made the long journey to Italy, 5,000 were despatched to the butchers through the Milan meat market.

The British Army had 25,000 horses in August 1914. It had taken only twelve days to increase that number to 165,000, acquired, entrained and delivered to the remount depots in the south of England. After that, the voracious appetite of the Army for horses was largely met by purchasing. Besides the nearly half a million which came from the United States, another 400,000 were bought at home, including 100,000 from Ireland. In the last year of the war, the army had more than 800,000 animals on its books, a quarter of them mules, mostly in Egypt and Mesopotamia, and in France, where they had become the mainstay of the supply chain.

The care the animals received produced an astonishingly low mortality rate – less than 14 per cent a year throughout the war and, notably, almost twice as good as the French managed to achieve. At the end of the war 200,000 horses were sold on the spot in France and Flanders and another 170,000 in the Middle East. From the army units in France 130,000 were sent back to Britain for sale. In France, almost a quarter of the animals went for meat.

Half a million horses and mules had died in the service of Britain and the Empire in the various theatres of war during those four years. A Yeomanry officer in Palestine told his own sad little tale of the war's end:

> Major Clayton had his own horse Columbus and Lieut. Leslie had Buzzie. I had my own very favourite Arab pony Reggie. At the end of the war, I, being junior, was left behind to clear up and do the unfortunate job of destroying the horses. We took them to the desert and shot them, as we did not want anyone to get them. But it was a very sad performance.

In all the dreadful statistics of the Great War, the death toll of men is beyond compare. But the carnage among horses, mules and even draft oxen was also meticulously recorded, though soon forgotten. Every week 3,000 died in the service of the British armies in France, in the battles with the Turks, even in Africa. The French armies saw twice as many die. In the August of 1917 there were 870,000 animals on the Army's roster. By the end of the year 60,000 of them were gone. The British Army had a large and skilled veterinary service which performed remarkably in keeping losses from wounds and disease to such a low level. At one point they were tending 90,000 patients. But still the vast majority of the horses died and, by the end of the war, of all the almost two million horses who had been drafted in to serve the colours, only about a quarter remained to be returned to civilian tasks. Many in the Middle East and Egypt were sold to often ill-suited local people, and their treatment became a furious scandal in the British press.

The toll of war was fearsome, but the end of war exacted its price too. The daunting level of attrition had encouraged horsemen to breed ever increasing numbers of animals to replace the endless casualties of the battlefield. But these foals were going to take four or five years to be ready for service. In 1916 the Ministry of Agriculture recorded the birth of 109,000 foals, but with the sudden arrival of peace in 1918 there was a precipitous collapse of demand for work horses of all sorts. In the first few months of 1919 the British Army unloaded a quarter

Red Cavalry, Kazimir Severinovich Malevich. (*State Russian Museum, St Petersburg, Russia/ Bridgeman Images*)

A Sale of Horses: Captured Turkish Ponies Sold at a Remount Depot, James McBey. (*Imperial War Museum, London, UK*)

of a million horses – mostly sold where they stood, 40,000 of them in France as well as nearly 10,000 mules. In Egypt 18,000 horses mules and donkeys – not to mention 20,000 camels – were sold to locals, many of them destined for the crushing workloads and unthinking brutality which was to arouse the pity of Dorothy Brooke just a few years later. Of the 10,000 horses bought in New Zealand and shipped off to the war zones, only four made it back, thanks to the stubborn determination of the officers who had ridden them. Captain Riddiford got Beauty home, as Captain Powles did Bess; General Sir Andrew Russell made sure his Dolly returned, and Nigger accompanied them, though her rider, Colonel George King, was dead.

In America there were 17,000 horses and mules awaiting shipment. They were all sold off – the mules fetching more than the horses. Though the British Army made more than £7 million from these sales, they exacerbated the collapse in the market.

The horse faded rapidly from the military – and indeed the artistic – mind, although the continuing civil war in Russia brought a last hurrah from Kazimir Malevich, with his picture of the Red Cavalry galloping distantly along a far horizon. Malevich had enthusiastically embraced the Revolution, launching the post-Futurist style which he called Suprematism and founding the Moscow Union of Painters.

In the Second World War the Allies actually used horses and, more particularly mules, in Italy to overcome the rocks and inclines which confronted them as they fought their way through the Apenines. Even in the twenty-first century, the American Army, sobered by some of the impassable landscapes of Afghanistan, did contemplate resurrecting its forgotten skills in mule and pack horse management.

The war had accelerated the decline of all forms of horsepower. Mechanical power was taking over, and economic factors played their part too. Within two years of the war's end a depression took hold that was almost as deep as the one which was to appear a decade later. In 1921 almost a fifth of British working men were without jobs. Farmland was being sold for £200 an acre, or even less. Shire stallions and mares, which had been selling at £1,000 or more at the end of the war, were fetching just £200 by 1923. It was simply impossible to sell most horses. A Midlands auctioneer later recalled selling only one animal out of a draft of fifty cart and carriage horses. The motor car, the tractor, the lorry and the tank, within but a few years, were to complete the obliteration of nearly all the tasks for which, in the desperate times of the Great War, the horse had been the lynchpin.

The War had been over more than a dozen years when a remarkable woman arrived in Egypt and established what was to prove the most practical and enduring of all the memorials to the horses of the Great War.

Dorothy Brooke was the wife of the cavalryman General Geoffrey Brooke, who was gazetted to command the British forces in Egypt in 1930. They were both horse lovers – indeed, he had ridden for Britain in the 1924 Olympics. They both soon heard of and saw the lamentable condition of former British war horses, now getting old but still toiling on the streets and in the quarries of Cairo and still bearing their British Army markings. In 1918, at the War's end, the decision had been taken, from fear of disease and excessive cost, that no horses should be sent home from the Middle East to Britain, Australia and New Zealand, though some went to India.

Dorothy Brooke started by buying a few of the frail horses she encountered. But soon, with money from friends and then, after a letter she had published in the London *Morning Post*, from well-wishers in Britain, the buying became a major undertaking. She described the moments when the horses were brought to the Old War Horse Memorial Hospital she set up in Cairo:

> As their ill-shod misshapen hooves felt the deep *tibbin* [chopped straw] bed beneath them, there would be a doubting, disbelieving, halt. Then gradually they would lower their heads and sniff as though they could not believe their own eyes and noses. Memories, long forgotten, would then return when some stepped eagerly forwards towards the mangers piled high with berseem [clover], while others, with creaking joints, lowered themselves slowly on to the bed and lay, necks and legs outstretched. There they remained, flat out, until hand fed by the *syces* [grooms].

Kindness, rest and comfortable surroundings were the guiding principles of Dorothy Brooke's hospital. But for the vast majority the ultimate kindness was judged to be a humane death. Only a few were returned to England.

In four years, Dorothy Brooke gathered in 5,000 veteran horses. But when that task came to an end, she threw her energies into establishing a hospital for the care of local horses in Cairo, and educating the owners in horse care. The Brookes were then posted to India, where a new series of hospitals came into being. Since then the Brooke animal hospitals have become one of the largest horse charities, with hospitals and programmes all round the globe.

At the end of the war there were more than 20,000 Australian horses in the Middle East. Only one of them reached home. He was Sandy, the mount of the Australian commander. All the rest were either sold, the majority to India, or shot.

Chapter 11

Resurrection

If there is a true temple of Remembrance in Britain to the Great War, it is the Sandham Chapel at Burghclere. The chapel was created by the sister of Lieutenant Henry Willoughby Sandham, who died at the end of the War. Mary Behrend and her husband Louis had commissioned Stanley Spencer to make a series of memorial paintings, and the chapel was designed specifically to display them, amid the lawns and orchards of Burghclere.

Spencer moved to Burghclere in 1926 and stayed until the final works were complete. Within the intimate white vaulting, the walls are full of Spencer's images, his fascination with the pertinence of the commonplace. Surrounded by his shattered troops, an officer concentrates on the details of his map. On the army hospital table the focus is on the piles of sliced bread. There are the practicalities of washing and dressing wounds. The harness and horse tackle are being diligently cleaned. And at the very centre, above the altar, is Spencer's *Resurrection*.

Amid the triumphantly redundant white crosses, as the once dead soldiers climb from the grave, there are two mules, still harnessed to their carts, arching their necks eagerly towards the new and heavenly life which evidently awaits them as well.

In all the altar pieces of the Christian churches across the world, there can be few, if any, where the joyous tidings of salvation are so clearly extended to the animal world.

Still fewer to the beasts of burden.

The Resurrection of the Soldiers, Stanley Spencer. (*Sandham Memorial Chapel, Burghclere, Hampshire, UK/ National Trust Photographic Library/A C Cooper/ Bridgeman Images*)